Dissenting Opinions

About The Author

Michael Sexton has degrees in law from the universities of Melbourne and Virginia. After some years as an academic lawyer and writer, he commenced practice as a barrister in the mid-1980s, taking silk in 1998. He currently holds the position of Solicitor General for New South Wales. He has been chairman of the NSW State Rail Authority and a board member of the NSW Public Transport Authority, the NSW State Library, the Sydney Writers' Festival and the University of Technology. He is the author of a number of legal texts and several books on politics and history, including:

Illusions of Power: The fate of a reform government (reissued as The Great Crash: The short life and sudden death of the Whitlam government)

War for the Asking: Australia's Vietnam Secrets (reissued as War for the Asking: How Australia invited itself to Vietnam)

The Regulation of Foreign Investment in Australia (with Alexander Adamovich)

The Legal Mystique: The role of lawyers in Australian society (with Laurence W Maher)

Australian Eyes Only

Australian Defamation Law and Practice (with T K Tobin QC)

Uncertain Justice: Inside Australia's Legal System

On the Edges of History: A Memoir of Law, Books and Politics

Dissenting Opinions

Michael Sexton

Connor Court Publishing

Published in 2020 by Connor Court Publishing Pty Ltd

Connor Court Publishing Pty Ltd
PO Box 7257
Redland Bay QLD 4165

sales@connorcourt.com
www.connorcourtpublishing.com.au
Phone 0497 900 685

ISBN: 9781 922 449 009

Front Cover Design: Maria Giordano
Front Cover Portrait: Brian Knox SC
Printed in Australia

CONTENTS

PREFACE

The term "dissenting opinions" is normally used in the law to describe the judgments of those members of appellate courts who take a different view in a particular case from their colleagues who form the majority and effectively decide the question before the court. I have used it, however, in relation to this collection of articles and book reviews published over several decades because they proposed in the main a departure from what might be characterised as the conventional wisdom, that is, the views and values of those who preside over most public and private intuitions in Australia, including much of the media.

I do not suggest for a moment that there has been any disadvantage to myself as a result of these publications but I have suggested in some of the pieces concerning the relatively recent phenomenon of political correctness that this climate of conformity has had a chilling effect on public debate. And that young people embarking on their careers now have to be wary of expressing unconventional opinions. This is even – and perhaps particularly – so in universities which historically were places where established ideas were always open to challenge.

Although some of these pieces are from earlier periods, most concern questions that are still controversial and can be taken as a contribution to those on-going discussions. Most importantly, however, they represent the hope that there will be much greater scope in the immediate future for the full-blooded public debate of social, economic and political issues in Australia.

Michael Sexton

May Day 2020

FREE SPEECH OR HATE SPEECH

A number of these pieces discuss the impact of section 18C of the federal Racial Discrimination Act 1975 which, amongst other things, makes it unlawful to publish material that is offensive to various groups in the community. No one suggests that public debate should normally be conducted by way of offense and insult but sometimes robust criticism of individuals and groups can offend their sensibilities, particularly if they are thin-skinned to start with. It should be noted that this is not just a problem of federal law because all States and Territories have somewhat similar legislative provisions that impinge on freedom of speech.

It is often said by the proponents of these statutes that they are designed to prevent "hate speech". But incitements to violence against any members of the community have always been a criminal offence and still are. What the supporters of provisions like section 18C describe as "hate speech" are often no more than statements with which they do not agree. As it happens, many offensive and insulting publications in recent times have been the work of those who condemn what they call hate speech.

Some of these pieces make particular reference to the current climate in universities which were historically bastions for freedom of speech but in more modern times have often been in the vanguard of the suppression of public discussion of controversial questions.

FREE SPEECH OR HATE SPEECH

THE AUSTRALIAN,

Tuesday, May 12, 2009

DEFEND TO THE LAST THEIR RIGHT TO SAY IT

Free speech means letting all opinions, no matter how offensive, be heard

In my days at the private Bar, when I did quite a bit of media law, people often came to see me wanting to sue in defamation over something that had been published about them. Sometimes I had to explain to them that the defence of fair comment was available for the publication because it seemed to be an expression of opinion on some facts that were set out by the writer. They were usually astonished. The idea that they could be attacked in the press without having any legal redress seemed an outrage.

This reaction reflects an attitude that is all too common in Australia. Almost everyone would, if asked, say that they were in favour of freedom of speech. But what they often mean is speech that they do not find offensive in any way.

There are various statutes that make it unlawful to publish material that is offensive to some groups in the community. One of this is the federal Racial Discrimination Act which may result in the imprisonment of Fredrick Toben, who posted material on the internet arguing that there was serious doubts that the Holocaust occurred. This is an absurd proposition and offensive not only to Jews but to anyone with the least knowledge of modern history. But that is not a reason to prevent Toben from expressing this utterly misguided view.

Proceedings were, however, taken against him – successfully – in the Federal Court by the Executive Council of Australian Jewry and in April he was found guilty of contempt, because he had not removed this material from the website where it had been published.

The sensitivities of a different group were offended in 2002 in Victoria when a number of Islamic converts brought proceedings against a Pentecostal Christian group under a State law that makes religious vilification unlawful. The case ran for five years in tribunals and courts before it was settled on confidential terms. It is hard to know what the American jurist Oliver Wendell Holmes would have made of all this. Writing a judgment in the US Supreme Court in 1919, he said:

> I think that we should be eternally vigilant against attempts to check the expression of opinions that we loathe and believe to believe to be fraught with death, unless they so imminently threaten immediate interference with the lawful and pressing purposes of the law that an immediate check is required to save the country.

Holmes' words do not, however, appear to have sunk in. In addition to these Australian examples, the Irish government announced plans at the end of April to make blasphemy a criminal offence, although presumably confined to attacks on Christian churches. In similar vein, the UN Human Rights Commission has proposed amending the UN Charter to outlaw the criticism of religious beliefs, by which its members essentially mean any criticism of the Islamic creed or its customs.

Earlier this month British authorities detained Dr Philip Nitschke, the Australian voluntary euthanasia campaigner, for nine hours when he arrived in London. No doubt there would be differing views in the community on Nitschke's opinion as to the desirability in some circumstances of a form of suicide (which is itself no longer a criminal offence). But why would the British government be concerned at anyone hearing those opinions? To quote Oliver Wendell Holmes again: "The best test of truth is the power of a thought to get itself accepted in the competition of the market".

Finally, what may seem like a trivial example, but one that perhaps illustrates the all too ready acceptance in this country of a range of restrictions on freedom of speech. In late April AFL CEO, Andrew Demetriou, said that there would be "zero tolerance" for any public criticism of umpires. Did I miss something here? I thought that umpires, like players, were public performers and fair game for criticism. But Hawthorn president, Jeff Kennett, was given the option of paying a $5,000 fine to the AFL or attending a re-education course with its umpiring department. Kennett chose to pay the fine rather than engage in such a degrading exercise.

The truth is that almost all countries have unnecessary restrictions on freedom of speech. The one general exception to this proposition is the United States, where a combination of the First Amendment and a long history of robust public debate has resulted in the practice of free speech not just its theory. The answer in Australia is not a Bill of Rights, because any right to freedom of speech in such legislation would be contradicted by rights not to be vilified on various grounds. The real answer is to accept that opinions, no matter how offensive to some or all members of the community, should be immune from all civil or criminal proceedings.

THE AUSTRALIAN,

Thursday, July 12, 2012

FROM SPORT TO THE MEDIA, WE MUST BE FREE TO OFFEND

In all aspects of life we have to stand up for the right of people we loathe to criticise us

"I hear the arguments about freedom of speech, but freedom of speech has to come with some responsibility. If we are all allowed to say everything we wanted to say, we'd be in a bit of strife…" So said AFL CEO Andrew Demetriou in mid-June after a number of Carlton players criticised some of the umpiring decisions on Twitter after their team's loss to West Coast in Perth. One of the players was sending on a tweet from his wife who had presumably been watching the game at home in Melbourne.

Demetriou seemed to compare these comments to racial vilification by saying that this was another example of unacceptable speech. He added that "we will not accept any criticism of umpires". Really? Don't they put on a public show like the players? Why can't they be the subject of comment?

The players were forced by Carlton to issue a public apology but this was not enough for the AFL which fined each of them $2,500. At the same time the review by the AFL umpiring department of the most controversial decision in the Perth game found it to be wrong.

All this came shortly after two swimmers on the Olympic team were told they would be sent home early from the Games in London in August after posting on Facebook a photograph of themselves with firearms in an American gun shop. Most people in Australia would probably favour close regulation of firearms and think that they are too readily available in the United States. But what has this got to do with the photograph in this case. Yes, it was juvenile and pointless, but so what?

At about the same time the Australian Olympic Committee hired a monitoring agency to send them text alerts if any athletes started placing negative material on Facebook or Twitter during the Games. The head of the monitoring agency mentioned security scares, transport snarls and disagreements between athletes as examples of negative stories that might surface.

There has never, of course, been any notion of free speech amongst most Australian sporting officials but this is just one example of a culture of control that would not be tolerated for a moment in the United States. When Andrew Demetriou says that speech can only be free if it is responsible, he sounded very like the Finkelstein inquiry into the media which rejected any traditional notion of free speech in the following terms:

> While it may be accepted that freedom of expression is important for self-fulfilment, it is not clear that unlimited free speech is essential for self-fulfilment … the speech that warrants protection is not all speech but 'that speech that is constitutive of the formation and planning of one's life in ways commensurate with one's informed conception of the good'.

Putting aside its almost unreadable style, the Finkelstein report started from the proposition that most members of the community are just not clever enough to make their own judgments about material published in the media without some guidance. The report said that, in order to engage in public debate, citizens must have the "relevant critical and speaking skills" but that there is "real doubt as to whether these capacities are present for all, or even most, citizens". This argument – that most people are stupid – is, of course, the argument of every anti-democrat in history, but the authors of the report, who obviously have no doubt that *they* possess the relevant "capacities," argue that regulation of speech is needed to *protect* democracy.

It is not necessary to like everything that Andrew Bolt writes to think that it is bad federal legislation that allows a newspaper article to be found unlawful simply because it might offend or insult some members of the community. And what is to be said about the Victorian legislation that makes it unlawful to engage in conduct that incites "serious ridicule" of a person or group of persons on the ground of religious beliefs or activities? No one likes being the subject of ridicule but it has always been a means of public debate and it only works if there is something ridiculous in the conduct that is attacked.

The very point about expressions of opinion that are offensive to some or even most members of the community is that they should be allowed despite their offensiveness. As the American jurist, Oliver Wendell Holmes said a century ago: "We should be eternally vigilant against attempts to check the expression of opinions that we loathe".

It is not the case, as Holmes went on to claim, that the truth will necessarily triumph in the "market" of ideas. But to live with the expressions of others that are untrue or unjust, or just silly, or that *we think* are untrue or unjust or silly, is one of the burdens of a democratic society, as well as of the human condition. The right response to speech that one finds offensive is one's own speech, not suppression.

THE AUSTRALIAN,
Monday, January 14, 2013

STATE LEGISLATION ALSO PUTS HURT FEELINGS ABOVE FREEDOM OF SPEECH

Those who value the right to robust debate should not just focus on federal laws

Most of the debate about freedom of speech in Australia has focused on proposed and existing federal legislation, particularly the provision of the Racial Discrimination Act that makes in unlawful to act in a way that is likely to offend, insult or humiliate a person on the basis of their race, colour, or national or ethnic origin.

It is important to remember, however, that four states have somewhat similar legislation that can raise questions of freedom of speech. In NSW, for example, the Anti-Discrimination Act makes it unlawful to "incite hatred towards, serious contempt for, or severe ridicule of" a person on the ground of race, transgender status, homosexuality or HIV-AIDS status.

Legislation in Victoria makes the same conduct unlawful in relation to matters of race and also on the ground of religious belief or activity. The Queensland statute refers to race, religion, sexuality and general identity. Tasmania targets race, disability, sexual orientation and religion.

The incitement of hatred – a very powerful emotion and, it might be thought, one difficult to really arouse – is arguably a suitable subject for regulation. But serious contempt may be a proper reaction to some conduct and severe ridicule has always been a legitimate debating tool.

These kinds of statutes usually, however, provide an exception for various publications. To use the NSW legislation again as an example, it exempts publications made for academic, artistic, scientific or research purposes or "for other purposes in the public interest, including discussion or debate about and expositions of any act or matter". Despite the opaque language of this last category, it would appear to cover political debate and public discussion of social and economic questions.

But there is a catch. The publications have to be made "reasonably and in good faith". Good faith presumably refers to the intentions of the speaker or writer, but reasonability is a subjective criterion. It may seem easy to say that the severe ridicule of an ostensibly vulnerable person or group is unreasonable but the whole point about expressions of opinion is that they should be protected even if they are unreasonable. If a publication gets the facts wrong, there is a remedy in the civil action of defamation. But the law of defamation provides a defence for expressions of opinion and this doesn't depend on the views being reasonable.

These principles have seldom been tested in cases under the legislation but they were canvassed in proceedings that arose out of an opinion article by Tom Switzer in the *Australian Financial Review* in December 1998 about the Middle East peace process, or lack of it. Among other things, Switzer said "the Palestinians cannot be trusted in the peace process" and that they "remain vicious thugs who show no serious willingness to comply with agreements". The AFR published a response by the Australian Arabic Council but the head of the Palestinian delegation in Australia, a substitute for a formal embassy in the absence of diplomatic recognition, brought proceedings for racial vilification in the NSW Administrative Decisions Tribunal.

The tribunal held that the article incited hatred of Palestinians and that the newspaper had not demonstrated that the publication was made reasonably and in good faith. On appeal, however, to the next level of the tribunal, the newspaper was successful. There was a finding that the commentator's statements referred to the Palestinian leadership and its involvement in the peace process rather than to the Palestinian people as a whole. In any event, according to the tribunal's appeals panel, the publication had been made for a purpose in the public interest discussion or debate about any subject, and it had been done reasonably and in good faith because the article was one of only a number of analyses of events in the Middle East in the newspaper before and after its appearance.

So this was a case where freedom of speech ultimately survived, although only after lengthy and costly legal proceedings. It is also true that the newspaper's case was probably easier to make out than the author's because the article was not its sole publication on the subject of the Middle East.

But this area of legislation indicates the potential problems with the use of such notions as offensiveness, insults, humiliation, contempt and ridicule. No one enjoys being the subject of this kind of literary invective. But the best response is to return fire. Hurt feelings, no matter how severe the wound, are not worth the sacrifice of freedom of speech.

THE AUSTRALIAN,

Tuesday, September 3, 2013

ROOM FOR OFFENSIVE VIEWS

Anti-BDS action attacks free speech

Universities have traditionally been thought of as bastions of free speech but three cases indicate that this is a rather fragile plant in the current climate of political discussion in Australia.

The most recent case concerns a complaint lodged with the federal Human Rights Commission against two academics at the Centre for Peace and Conflict Studies at Sydney University. The complaint has been lodged by a group of Israeli lawyers and is based on the academics' support for the so-called BDS campaign. BDS – standing for boycott, divestment and sanctions – was established in July 2005 by a number of Palestinian organisations and targets the products of Israeli business enterprises and those of international corporations that are said to profit from the violation of Palestinian rights. It is also aimed at Israeli sporting, cultural and academic institutions. In Australia there have been a number of BDS demonstrations at Max Brenner chocolate cafes on the ground that it is a franchise of the Israeli-based Strauss food and beverage group.

The complaint to the Human Rights Commission is based on the federal Racial Discrimination Act. Complaints before the Commission are the subject of a process of conciliation but, if that is unsuccessful, they can be taken to the Federal Court in the same way that Andrew Bolt was the subject of proceedings – also under the Racial Discrimination Act – because of his statements about a number of prominent aboriginals.

The relevant provision of the Racial Discrimination Act makes it unlawful to "do any act involving a distinction, exclusion, restriction or preference based on race, colour, descent or national or ethnic origin" that has the purpose or effect of nullifying or impairing any human right or fundamental freedom. This wording arguably raises more questions that it answers but presumably the complaint in this case alleges conduct based on Israeli national origin or Jewish race or ethnic origin. In fact, the promotion of the boycott appears to be based on political opposition to the Israeli position and not the grounds identified in the legislation.

I have written occasionally on the Middle East, broadly in support of Israel, and I imagine these views would be highly unattractive to supporters of BDS. But, if freedom of speech means anything, it means the freedom to put forward views that are highly offensive to some groups and, on occasions, to almost all members of the community. Why shouldn't it be possible to argue for the boycott of Japanese cars on the basis of that country's whaling policies or the boycott of Chinese clothing imports on the ground of China's indifference to the rights and freedoms present in most Western countries? These kinds of campaigns have traditionally been ineffective but that is not a reason to prohibit them.

The use of bodies like the Human Rights Commission and the Federal Court to stifle the publication of political views, however distasteful they might be to some sections of society, underlines again the dangers of legislation that allows and encourages these kinds of attacks on freedom of speech.

Early this year Sydney University was the subject of another debate about freedom of speech when it emerged that it has a formal policy that prohibits behaviour that would offend, insult or humiliate persons on such grounds as age, sex, political opinion, sexuality or religion. The penalties for breach of the policy by students include suspension, expulsion or fines. No one would normally want to encourage conduct that is insulting or humiliating of individuals but sometimes this is the stuff of political debate. And the notion that offensive statements in the course of exchanges on social and political questions could lead to suspension or expulsion seems completely antithetical to the idea of a university.

The same might be said of the reaction of the Australian National University in May of this year to a satirical article in its student newspaper that described a passage from the Koran as a "rape fantasy". The article was the last of a series of satires about religions that had previously dealt with Catholicism, Scientology, Mormonism and Judaism. There didn't seem to be any problem about lampooning these beliefs. But in this last case the university administration forced the editors of the newspaper to pulp the material after threatening them with expulsion from the university and the withdrawal of the publication's funding.

These cases all concern universities but there are many areas in Australia where tolerance of strong opinions is confined by many people to those opinions with which they happen to agree. There is too much legislation at both the federal and State level that encourages this blinkered outlook on the world. A review of this legislation is long overview and might stimulate a more robust debate in this country on major public issues.

THE AUSTRALIAN,

Monday, March 3, 2014

WE ALL HAVE A RIGHT TO FREE SPEECH AND IT SHOULD BE NO CRIME TO OFFEND

Offensive statements are legitimate tools of debate

Late last year in these columns I complained that it was very difficult in Australia to have a debate about freedom of speech because those who wanted to restrict that freedom would hardly ever break cover and make their views public. Not for the first time, you need to be careful what you wish for. The federal government's campaign promise to amend section 18C of the Commonwealth Racial Discrimination Act has unleashed some strong opposition from ethnic groups, including the Hellenic Council, the Chinese Australian Forum, the Arab Council and the Council of Australian Jewry.

It is worth recalling just what section 18C actually makes unlawful. It refers to conduct that "is reasonably likely, in all the circumstances, to offend, insult, humiliate or intimidate another person or a group of people" because of the race, colour or national or ethnic origin of the other person or some or all of the people in the group. It is true that an exemption is provided for expressions of opinion on matters of public interest but this is completely undermined by the requirement that these statements must be made "reasonably".

There is room for argument as to whether the prohibition on intimidation should be retained, although this could normally be dealt with by the ordinary provisions of the criminal law. The notions of offence, insult and humiliation, however, involve hurt to feelings. This is always unattractive for the subject of the verbal attack but these shock tactics have always been legitimate tools of debate on questions of politics and public interest. Sometimes these attacks are totally unreasonable. But there should be no place in a federal or State statute for a prohibition on their use in public discussion of social and economic issues.

One of the arguments put by the defenders of section 18C is that it was used to bring proceedings in the Federal Court over a period of ten years against Fredrick Toben who denies there is evidence that the Holocaust took place in the late 1930s and early 1940s. Toben's claim is, of course, absurd and naturally offensive to Jewish members of the community. But that is no reason for stopping him expressing this view. The right response to speech that one finds offensive is one's own speech, not suppression. There are many examples of distortions of history. Should Turkish diplomats around the world, including those in Australia, be the subject of proceedings under section 18C because they vehemently deny that up to a million Armenians were killed in Turkey in 1916, when all the available evidence indicates that this is what happened?

Some of the defenders of section 18C describe it as a bulwark against "hate speech". One problem about this term is that it is now frequently used with reference to publications that are merely offensive. Hatred is a very powerful emotion and one, it might be thought, relatively rarely encountered. The Commonwealth Criminal Code already makes unlawful statements urging the use of force or violence against a person or group distinguished by their race, religion, nationality, national or ethnic origin or political opinion. This is an offence punishable by imprisonment for up to seven years if the use of the force or violence would threaten the peace, order and good government of the Commonwealth and otherwise by imprisonment for up to five years.

If it be thought necessary to outlaw incitements to "hatred" that somehow fall short of the urging or force or violence – historically a rare form of publication in our society – it would be possible to include the kind of provision present, for example, in the NSW

Anti-Discrimination Act that makes the incitement of hatred on the grounds of race an offence. This provision refers to threatening physical harm and inciting others to threaten harm, but it is not limited to these forms of conduct. There is always a danger, however, that, in the absence of incitements to violence, these kinds of provisions will be used to stifle publications that are merely offensive.

It is hardly surprising that this is an area of particular sensitivity in some sections of the Jewish community. In the aftermath of the Holocaust the state of Israel was established as the only democracy in the Middle East. Despite this history, hostility to Israel is an article of faith in large sections of the media and universities in Europe and in Australia. The BDS boycott movement is just one manifestation of this underlying view.

It would, however, be a pity if representatives of the Jewish community in Australia allowed themselves to be used as part of a campaign to stop the repeal of section 18C. In the long run they have the same interest in freedom of speech as everyone else. As the American jurist Oliver Wendell Holmes said more than a century ago: "We should be eternally vigilant against attempts to check the expressions of opinions we loathe."

THE AUSTRALIAN,

Monday, January 12, 2015

THOSE WHO SAY THEY ARE CHARLIE SHOULD SUPPORT CHANGES TO 18C

The satirical journalists and cartoonists died defending the right to give offence

One thing seems to have been hardly mentioned in the extensive coverage in this country of the Paris killings – that the reason for the attack was that the cartoons in *Charlie Hebdo* mocking Islam were offensive to some members of that community and that offensive publications were at the heart of the debate in Australia over section 18C of the federal Racial Discrimination Act.

Does anyone remember that section 18C makes it unlawful to publish material that is reasonably likely to offend or insult a person or a group of persons where this is done on the basis of race, colour or national or ethnic origin? It is true that there is an exception for material published "reasonably and in good faith" as part of discussions in the public interest or a fair comment on a matter of public interest. But these are judgments that will be made initially by the Australian Human Rights Commission and ultimately by a judge of the Federal Court. Who would want to take the risk that their offensive or insulting material will be found to have been published reasonably and in good faith in the subjective view of these bodies?

Everyone, of course, says that they are in favour of freedom of speech but many of the pious platitudes to this effect uttered in Australia in the wake of the Paris attack have been made by persons and groups that vehemently opposed the federal government's proposal to repeal or amend section 18C. There are, in fact, a lot of people who don't believe in freedom of speech at all – except for the expression of opinions that accord with their own.

Normally opponents of freedom of speech keep a low profile. They move behind the scenes to have provisions like section 18C put on the statute book but then prefer to leave their enforcement to the AHRC and the courts. When the federal government proposed changes to section 18C, however, many of these groups broke cover and fiercely defended its existing terms. The federal Attorney General was deluged with lengthy submissions from ethnic groups, legal professional bodies and so-called community organisations arguing that section 18C was all that protected minority groups from oppression in Australian society. The truth is that Australia has an enviable record of racial and religious tolerance that had survived even the tireless efforts of those bodies – all publicly funded – that spend their time trying to find examples of intolerance in order to justify their continued existence.

The debate over freedom of speech is sometimes confused by references to "hate speech". In many quarters this is simply a reference to views with which the speaker disagrees. There can be, of course, incitements to violence against particular persons or groups but this is an offence punishable by imprisonment up to five years under the Commonwealth Criminal Code. The incitement of hatred, without any suggestion of violence, is more problematic. It might be thought that such publications are relatively rare, given how unusual genuine hatred is as an emotion. They are highly undesirable but there is a danger that attempts to deal with them can be used to ban publications that are merely offensive.

No one likes being the subject of offensive or insulting attacks but these have always been legitimate tools of debate on political and social questions. There should be no place in Australia for a prohibition on their use in public discussions of these kinds of issues. The journalists in Paris were killed because they published offensive material. The defenders of section 18C no doubt deplore what happened but they would not approve of the publication of the offensive cartoons.

THE AUSTRALIAN,

Thursday, November 26, 2015

THE FREEDOM TO OFFEND ALLOWS PUBLIC DEBATE ON LIFE'S BIGGEST ISSUES

Restricting free speech poses real problems for churches and religious groups

The problem of how freedom of speech is restricted by some federal and State legislation has been raised again by a decision of the Tasmanian Anti-Discrimination Commissioner.

The Commission found that the Catholic Church has a case to answer over its distribution of a booklet to the parents of Catholic school students supporting traditional marriage. A complaint had been lodged with the Commission by a transgender person who argued the booklet contravened the provision of the Tasmanian Anti-Discrimination Act that makes it unlawful to offend, humiliate, intimidate, insult or ridicule a person on the basis of various attributes. Those attributes include, for the purposes of this case, sexual orientation, marital status and relationship status. It is necessary that a reasonable person would have anticipated that the subject of the conduct in question would be offended, humiliated, intimidated, insulted or ridiculed.

All this is reminiscent of s 18C of the federal Racial Discrimination Act which makes it unlawful to offend or insult racial, national and ethnic groups in the community, although that provision does not even have the qualification that a reasonable person would regard the conduct or publication as offensive or insulting. The contest over the repeal of s 18C was, of course, lost by the proponents of freedom of speech. There is no real point in revisiting that issue at present because the federal government has clearly indicated that it is not going to change the decision made by former Prime Minister Abbott.

But the Tasmanian legislation – and similar legislation in some of the other States and Territories – poses real problems on its face for churches and other religious groups. To take an example, as anyone who has read *Brideshead Revisited* will recall, it is Catholic teaching that unmarried heterosexual couples are "living in sin" and so doomed to the eternal fires of hell. Why is it not open to such a couple to complain that they are offended and insulted by church publications to this effect because those publications are made on the basis of their relationship status? It would then be up to the Church to argue that a reasonable person would not have this reaction but that decision might depend very much on the personal views of the Anti-Discrimination Commissioner.

What all this shows is that, once the principle of freedom of speech is undermined, it is easy to find any number of persons who are offended or insulted by the views of others. This is not to say that incitements to violence, for example, against particular groups in the community should not be unlawful. This kind of conduct has in fact always been unlawful under the criminal law. But it is very different from expressions of opinion that may be offensive or insulting.

It is not only in Australia that freedom of speech is under threat. In many American universities administrators have come under pressure from some staff and students to abandon course material that might offend some groups. In some cases teachers have been required to warn the students that class content might offend them so that the students can absent themselves and avoid this terrible fate. This climate of fear reached new levels just before Halloween at Yale University when administrators sent an email to students advising them not to wear certain kinds of costumes so as to avoid offending others. When the wife of the master of one of the University's residential colleges suggested that the way to deal with offensive conduct was to ignore it, some of the students mounted an attack on her husband. As one student said, the university was "not about creating an intellectual space" where conflicting opinions could be expressed. It might be thought that for many centuries that is exactly what a university was about – a place for a robust exchange of ideas even if some peoples' feelings were hurt in the debate. But there are obviously students now at Yale who reject that long-held view.

To return to the Tasmanian case, most people in Australia do not subscribe to the teachings of the Catholic Church but that is no reason why the Church and other religious bodies should not be able to advance their moral teachings without being subject to lengthy and costly legal proceedings. If there is no freedom to offend, there can be no genuine public debate, not only on religious questions but also on many political and social issues.

THE AUSTRALIAN,

Tuesday, March 1, 2016

CURBS ON GIVING OFFENCE CAN STIFLE PUBLIC DEBATE

Arguing against same-sex marriage would be unlawful in some jurisdictions

A Christian group has been heavily criticised by a number of commentators because they raised the question of whether it would be necessary for the Commonwealth to override areas of State and Territory legislation if a plebiscite on same-sex marriage were to take place. But there are various laws in these jurisdictions that could make it unlawful for bodies opposed to same-sex marriage to put their case to the electorate.

Take the example of the Tasmanian Anti-Discrimination Act, not least because it has already been used to bring legal proceedings against the Catholic Church over its distribution of a booklet supporting traditional marriage to the parents of Catholic school students. This legislation makes it unlawful to offend, humiliate, intimidate, insult or ridicule a person on the basis of various attributes. Those attributes include sexual orientation, marital status and relationship status, provided a reasonable person would have anticipated that the subject of the conduct in question would be offended or otherwise affected.

It would, therefore, be open to persons in same-sex relationships to complain that they had been offended by a "No" campaign in the course of the plebiscite that argued that same-sex marriage was sinful in a religious sense or simply socially undesirable. These views may not represent those of a majority in the community but that is no reason why they should not be allowed to be put to the electorate. This is why the proposed plebiscite throws into sharp relief the problems of this kind of legislation in a way that individual cases may not. Laws that make it unlawful to offend various groups in the community inevitably stifle public debate on contentious social, economic and political issues. This is because some people will always be offended if their lifestyles or their views are criticised or disparaged.

Proponents of these kinds of laws suggest that they are necessary to prevent "hate speech". No one argues that incitements to violence against particular sections of the community should not be unlawful. As it happens, this kind of conduct has always been an offence under the criminal law. This is real "hate speech" but it is a far cry from expressions of opinion that may be offensive to some persons when made in the course of a vigorous political debate.

Of course freedom of speech is not an absolute value. It has always been subject to many qualifications including the law of defamation – to protect individual reputation – and the law of contempt – to protect the administration of justice. But this is very different from a restriction on speech that is designed to protect a person's feelings from being offended.

The rationale underlying these laws has been taken to the extreme position in some American universities where lecturers have been required to warn students about passages in textbooks that they might find offensive. No doubt there will be a move to follow suit by some zealous staff in the history and international relations departments of universities in this country. Universities were once thought of as the very places where the existing views of students – and teachers – could be challenged fearlessly. But once freedom of speech is curtailed in this way there is no reason to allow any contrary views to be heard.

Even assuming that the Commonwealth could quarantine State legislation in this area for the purposes of a plebiscite on same-sex marriage, it would face even greater difficulties in the case of a referendum on the recognition of indigenous people in the Constitution. The reason is that the Commonwealth's own s 18C of the Racial Discrimination

Act makes it unlawful to offend racial, national and ethnic groups. It is certainly possible that arguments against amending the Constitution in this way for whatever reason might be offensive to Aboriginal organisations involved in supporting a referendum.

How have we got to the position in Australia where laws might have to be suspended so that there can be a proper public discussion of a serious social and political issue in a plebiscite or a referendum? Doesn't it suggest that such laws have the ability at all times to inhibit the freedom of speech without which these issues cannot be fully debated in this country?

THE SPECTATOR AUSTRALIA

8 October 2016

ON THE HATERS AND THEIR HATRED OF 'HATE SPEECH'

In the law of libel a statement of claim still alleges, as it has for centuries, that the plaintiff has been brought into "hatred, ridicule and contempt" by the publication in question.

Until recently this was one of the rare references to hatred in modern times. This might be thought hardly surprising, given that such a violent emotion would normally be seldom encountered. But it seems that Australian society is now awash with "hate speech" – a term inherited from the United States and originally referring to incitements to violence against minority groups. It has now, however, in both countries, been taken over by the politically correct class to mean various views on social and economic questions with which they disagree.

So the heading of the *Sydney Morning Herald* editorial on the eve of the European Union vote in Britain was: "A victory for hate if Brexit should prevail". In the *Herald's* cartoon of the prime minister speaking about refuges at the United Nations in the last week of September he was shown as wearing three badges inscribed with the following words:

- "Hate makes the world go round"
- "Hate will find a way"
- "All you need is hate"

When two members of the Senate earlier this year proposed the amendment of section 18C of the federal Racial Discrimination Act they were described by the *Herald* as "hate-speech apologists".

In addition Senator David Leyonhjelm was said to be "a boorish, supercilious know-all with the empathy of a Besser block". His colleague, Senator Malcolm Roberts, was referred to as "an absurdist fringe-dweller". Both were finally portrayed as "self-promoting misanthropes". If the proponents of section 18C are to be believed, it is the only thing standing between minority groups in Australia and a tidal wave of the vilest forms of vilification.

The truth is that most of the vitriolic abuse occurring in public debate in Australia comes from the politically correct class and reflects their almost disbelieving response to an alternative point of view. In the course of their constant and confected concerns about hate speech they have themselves determined to make any opponents the subject of libel law's hatred, ridicule and contempt.

It might be noted that incitement to violence against any group in the community, although almost unknown in Australian history, has always been an offence under the criminal law. It was, of course, sanctioned by the law in Germany in the 1930s but that has never been the case in any other Western country. It is hardly an incitement to violence to raise, for example, questions about immigration into Australia – its level, composition, costs and benefits – but anyone who does so is instantly accused of hate speech by the forces of political correctness.

This is the same mindset that has now discovered that many works of history and classical literature contain passages that might offend the sensitivities of some individuals who come across them. This set off a demand in many American universities that students be warned in advance about such passages in their prescribed texts so that they can avoid the immense psychological damage that might be caused by reading them. Needless to say, this trend has been picked up in a number of Australian universities and, these institutions being themselves bastions of political correctness, such demands have been taken seriously and, in some cases, accepted.

The visiting American novelist Lionel Shriver, was exposed to these sensitivities when she gave the opening address to the Brisbane Writers' Festival in September. Shriver had said that fiction writers naturally wrote not only about their own personal experience but also created characters from different backgrounds to their own. Some minority groups protested and the Festival immediately disowned Shriver and organised a "right of reply" session. Shriver has been accused of being a racist – the instant reaction by the politically correct class to expressions of opinion on so many social and economic questions. Shriver probably did not realise that all cultural institutions in Australia, including literary festivals, are also bastions of political correctness. She knows now.

Naturally the government's proposed plebiscite on same-sex marriage has provoked claims that it would unleash an avalanche of hate speech from those who are opposed to any change in the definition of marriage. It is obviously an available argument to say that a parliamentary vote is preferable to a plebiscite on any particular issue. But it is rather different to contend that a legitimate subject for public debate cannot even be discussed.

We can expect to hear a lot more about hate speech in the immediate future as the chief fomenters of hatred in Australian society label any disagreement with their views in this fashion. Discovering hate speech has become a big industry in the US and looks set to be even bigger here.

THE AUSTRALIAN,

Monday, October 2, 2017

INJURED FEELINGS JUST THE PRICE OF FREE SPEECH DURING A SERIOUS DEBATE

Anti-discrimination laws rely on subjective interpretations of the phrase 'in good faith'

The same-sex marriage postal vote has raised – yet again - the problem of laws that make it unlawful to publish material that is said to be offensive or insulting to various groups in the community.

The battle over s 18C of the federal Racial Discrimination Act was, of course, lost by proponents of free speech. But the thing to remember about that provision is that it makes it unlawful to publish material that is offensive to individuals or groups, on the basis of their race, colour or national or ethnic origin, even if the publication would not be considered offensive by ordinary members of society but is considered offensive by especially sensitive members of one of these groups.

All States and both Territories have anti-discrimination legislation that makes unlawful publications concerning racial groups but also extends the law to a much wider range of publications. The broadest of these statutes is the Tasmanian Anti-Discrimination Act. This legislation makes it unlawful to offend, humiliate, intimidate, insult or ridicule a person on the basis of various attributes. Those attributes include sexual orientation, marital status and relationship status, provided a reasonable person would have anticipated that the subject of the conduct in question would be offended or otherwise affected.

This would appear to leave it open to persons in same-sex relationships to complain to the Anti-Discrimination Commissioner that they were offended by advertisements put forward by the "No" campaign that suggested, for example, that children were disadvantaged when brought up by same-sex parents as opposed to different-sex parents. And a reasonable person may well have anticipated that same-sex parents would be offended by such a claim.

It might be noted that it would also seem open to unmarried different-sex couples to complain about the traditional teaching of Christian churches which says that living together without marriage is – to use a very old-fashioned expression – sinful. There have, however, been no such complaints, which suggest that such couples are not overly sensitive about the notion of living in sin.

Like most of its State and Territory counterparts, the Tasmanian legislation provides a defence to an otherwise unlawful publication if it is done "in good faith" for a purpose in the public interest. It might be thought that this would protect publications made in the course of a discussion of political and social issues but there are two problems about this. The first is that the notion of good faith is a very subjective one and is left up to the tribunal or court hearing a complaint. The second problem is that, as the Queensland University of Technology students discovered when they were the subject of a complaint to the federal Human Rights Commission, there is little point in such a defence if it can only be made out after years of litigation and the expenditure of large sums on legal costs.

There is an obvious potential for this kind of legislation to be used – or abused – during the postal vote campaign in an attempt to stop media advertisements or public speeches. It might be argued that such State and Territory legislation does not extend to campaign publications because new Commonwealth legislation on this subject covers the field and so overrides the operation of these State and Territory statutes. This is a difficult constitutional question and would have to be determined by a court.

But, even if that argument is right, there may still be problems with the new Commonwealth law. The legislation would make it illegal to vilify, intimidate or threaten to harm a person either because of the views they hold on the postal vote or in relation to their religious conviction, sexual orientation, gender identity or intersex status. It is hard to imagine a television advertisement that intimidates or threatens to harm anyone but vilification is an easy allegation to make and there is a danger that it would provide media organisations with an excuse to reject confronting advertising material.

No one suggests that real "hate speech" – incitements to violence against sections of the community – should not be unlawful, as they always have been under the criminal law. But this is very different from expressing opinions in the course of a serious political debate that some people may find offensive. Laws that restrict those kinds of opinions inevitably stifle public debate on political and social questions because some persons will always be offended if their lifestyles or views are criticised. But injured feelings may sometimes be the price of freedom of speech.

THE AUSTRALIAN,

Tuesday, May 29, 2018

CHURCHES COUNTING ON EXEMPTIONS TO KEEP PREACHING WHAT THEY PRACTISE

Anti-discrimination laws threaten freedom of speech, and not just for religious bodies

The Ruddock inquiry into religious freedom, instituted by the federal government in the wake of the legislation authorising same sex marriage, has completed its work but its findings have not been made public yet. In many ways the real issue is one of freedom of speech and is not a problem confined to religious bodies.

The recent case of rugby star Israel Folau illustrates some of the difficulties in this area. It should be said at the outset that Folau's public statements on the question of same sex marriage do no more than reflect the traditional teachings of some Christian churches on this subject. They hardly constitute a form of hate speech, despite the hyperbole of some commentators. These views are no doubt uncommon today but it may be noted that the same traditional teachings regard couples of different sex in a relationship outside marriage as living in sin. Readers of Evelyn Waugh's *Brideshead Revisted* will recall how seriously these concepts were taken at one time by members of more mainstream religious bodies.

It has been said that the complaints of some of the Rugby Australia sponsors about Folau's statements raise an issue of freedom of speech. But it is a fact – sad or otherwise – of modern Australian life that a highly paid sportsman or sportswoman cannot continue to make public statements, especially unfashionable ones on moral questions, that alienate sponsors and expect to survive, given the views that dominate almost all public institutions in this country and the boards of most large corporations.

But the real issue of freedom of speech in this area is whether churches will be able to continue their traditional teachings in pulpits and schools in the light of state and territorial legislation that makes it illegal to engage in conduct that offends or otherwise injures the feelings of individuals on the basis of, for example, their participation in same sex marriage.

Tasmanian anti-discrimination legislation is the most comprehensive of these statutes and prohibits such conduct on the basis of, amongst other things, sexual orientation, sexual activity, gender, gender identity, marital status and relationship status.

There is obviously considerable room here for some persons to be offended by what they see as the churches' condemnation of their lifestyle and to file complaints with the anti-discrimination commissioner on the basis of sermons or teaching materials. As is well-known from the litigation of complaints under section 18C of the federal Racial Discrimination Act, there are some defences available under this kind of legislation but, even if complaints are ultimately unsuccessful, they inevitably involve the subject of the complaint in considerable time, expense and personal stress.

This is presumably one of the issues considered by the Ruddock inquiry. The reason that this question looms large is that there is no exception for religious teaching in the various statutory provisions dealing with conduct that offends individuals on the basis of conditions such as sexual preference, marital status or relationship status. Other conduct by religious institutions is normally exempted from the provisions of anti-discrimination legislation. So the Tasmanian statute allows discrimination on the ground of gender if required by the doctrines of the religious institution in question and allows discrimination in relation to employment if the participation of the potential employee in the observance or practice of a particular religion is a genuine occupational qualification or requirement. In particular, discrimination is permitted in relation to employment in an educational institution conducted in accordance with the teachings of a religion if the discrimination is to enable the educational institution to conduct itself with those teachings.

There has been, of course, increasing opposition from some groups in the community to the existence of these exemptions but so far they largely have survived in this kind of legislation.

The provisions in anti-discrimination legislation that make offensive statements illegal do not, of course, cause a problem for religious teachings only. As with section 18C, they have the potential to stifle robust public debate on a wide range of social, economic and political questions, given the readiness of some members of the community to take offence at any publications that criticise their views or activities.

Naturally this suits the guardians of political correctness who do not want public debate on many of these issues.

As for Folau, he could be worse off. He could be still playing in the AFL – the most politically correct of all the sporting bodies, and, perhaps not incidentally, the least ethnically diverse of the three codes Folau has played and the one with no international component – in which case he would already be out of a job.

THE AUSTRALIAN,
Friday, March 29, 2019

THE MOST EASILY OFFENDED CAN BE THE MOST OFFENSIVE

Of course we must all be able to speak freely, but you can't have it both ways

We hear a great deal today about "hate speech" and it is worth remembering that the genuine article – incitements to violence against individuals or particular groups in the community – have always been criminal offences under the common law. It is, however, not the same as statements made in the course of public debate that may be offensive.

This is not to say that discussion of economic, social and political issues should normally be conducted in a way that is deliberately offensive but some groups are easily offended and this is a price that may have to be paid if freedom of speech is to be truly valued.

This kind of speech, usually categorised as offensive or insulting in legislation, is, however, made unlawful by s 18C of the federal Racial Discrimination Act and by anti-discrimination legislation in most of the States and Territories. Those statutory provisions are fiercely defended as a proper restriction on freedom of speech by the most politically correct members of the community. But it is something of an irony that many of these opponents of offensiveness in some areas specialise in particularly offensive statements against their political opponents.

Sydney University appears to be a special source of this kind of virulent rhetoric. In 2018 one of its history professors asked whether *The Australian's* Greg Sheridan and Chris Kenny "think that Western countries are succumbing to a poisonous cocktail of multiculturalism, Muslim immigration, political correctness and cultural Marxism" adding: "It seems that, much like Anders Breivik and Steve Bannon, they do." What is to be made of a comparison between the mindset of these two journalists and the Norwegian mass-murderer?

Then in the wake of the Christchurch killings, a member of the University's literature department wrote in the *Sydney Morning Herald* that the great books program of the Ramsay Centre for Western Civilisation provides a reason "to reflect on how the Ramsay curriculum validates the world view behind the massacre." In the same week the University's student newspaper, *Honi Soit*, published a cartoon on its cover of Cardinal George Pell hanging from a noose and covered in blood. The editors of the papers responded to criticisms by stating that the cartoon was "a visual allegory that strongly and unequivocally condemns one individual for their own vile acts" This is the same student journal that in May 2018 carried a photo on its cover of a female suicide bomber who had killed many Israelis, describing her as a "martyr" in the struggle against "Israeli colonisation."

In March 2018 Julian Burnside, now the Greens candidate in the forthcoming federal election for the seat of Kooyong in Melbourne's eastern suburbs, posted on Twitter an image of the federal Minister for Home Affairs, Peter Dutton in a Nazi uniform. Burnside is no fringe dweller on social media but a Queens Counsel at the Victorian Bar and a member of the Order of Australia. It is a measure of how far political debate has deteriorated in Australia that a person of Burnside's status in the community would descend to this level of common abuse. It is almost unthinkable that this would have occurred even 20 years ago. This kind of hyperbole has been mirrored in the US where, for example, a column by Max Boot in the *Washington Post* in January of this year claimed that President Trump's views were "almost indistinguishable" from those of a white supremacy advocate and added that he "created a climate of rhetorical violence that has been associated with mail bombs and a synagogue shooting."

If one really believes in freedom of speech, it is not necessary to share these kinds of histrionic views to agree that they should not be censored, let alone made unlawful. As the American jurist Oliver Wendell Holmes said in a Supreme Court judgment in 1919: "I think that we should be eternally vigilant against attempts to check the expression of opinions that we loathe and believed to be fraught with death, unless they so imminently threaten immediate interference with the lawful and pressing purposes of the law that an immediate check is required to save the country."

All this reflects a situation where many of the greatest defenders of legislative restrictions on offensive publications are themselves practitioners of wildly offensive speech. That should be their right but, selectively, they want some groups within the protection of the law but others well beyond its protection. The only freedom of speech they really believe in is their own.

THE WORLD OF POLITICAL CORRECTNESS

The American economist, John Kenneth Galbraith, coined the phrase "the conventional wisdom" in the 1960s. So he would have recognised the development in Australia over recent decades of a conventional wisdom on a whole range of subjects. This is now better known as the phenomenon of political correctness and is rigidly policed by large sections of the media; most teaching staff in schools and universities; legal professional bodies; the boards of many large corporations; the federal and State bureaucracies; and the major sporting codes.

The following articles describe this system of conformity but also speculate as to how this situation came about in a relatively short space of time, probably only over the last 25 years. Just how these powerful bodies in our society were captured by the forces of political correctness is not easy to explain, although the huge expansion of universities over this period and changing school curriculums may provide part of the answer. Whatever the reasons, however, there can be little doubt that political correctness has had a significant impact on the willingness of individuals to participate in public debate on important social, political and economic issues in Australia.

THE WORLD OF POLITICAL CORRECTNESS

THE AUSTRALIAN,

Wednesday, July 24, 2013

WRITERS FESTIVALS AN ECHO CHAMBER OF OPINIONS

Audiences are unlikely to have their biases challenged at literary and cultural events

The Sydney Writers Festival in my time had a mixture of public funding, corporate sponsorship and private donations. Any public funding carries, of course, some responsibilities. Gerard Henderson has pointed out that there is not a great deal of diversity in the social and political views of the writers and media commentators appearing at recent Sydney Writers Festivals. This is largely true, as it is for the Melbourne Festival. I have not examined the programs for other festivals around the country but I imagine that a similar criticism could be made in most cases. In explaining this phenomenon – as opposed to defending it – it needs to be remembered that institutions are a product of their societies and literary festivals in Australia are a product of a part of Australian society – publishers, writers, bureaucrats and the media – that largely shares a common view on most social and political questions. There are quite a number of persons in all of those groups who hold sharply different views but they represent a minority position.

There is not much doubt about the fact of this consensus but the reasons for it are more difficult to divine. When I was at university in the late 1960s – seemingly some time ago but not long by historical standards – most corporate managers, senior bureaucrats and lawyers together with a good proportion of academics and journalists were sympathetic to the US's role in the world; to the actions of the police and other law enforcement bodies in dealing with crime; to policies designed to secure the country's borders; and to some limits on government regulation. Those groups now largely hold almost exactly the opposite opinions. They are still, of course, at the heart of the establishment but somehow see themselves as a moral minority. This was a development identified by Nick Cater in his book *The Lucky Culture*, published earlier this year. The turnaround does explain the programs at literary festivals. This is because, as I have already suggested, literary festivals are organised by a relatively small segment of our society. The views that I have referred to earlier are not widely held in the general community but they are held by those groups that occupy Australia's cultural worlds, one of which, using the word in its broadest sense, is the media.

Having said all that, it has always seemed to me that even these groups would have more fun at festivals and other events if there were sometimes real debate on social and political questions; that is, some robust disagreement between the presenters, with the audience able to ultimately join in and express their opinions. This is not, of course, just a problem for literary festivals. If it ever did, Australia certainly does not now have the tradition of vigorous public debate that has always existed in the US. There are plenty of criticisms that can be made of the US political system but there is a much wider range of ideas open for discussion than in the relatively narrow spectrum of Australian politics. And the same can be said about a wide variety of social and economic issues about which it is difficult to spark any debate in Australia.

To give one example – over the last year or so there has been some criticism of legislation at the federal and State level in this country that criminalises expressions of opinion offensive to individuals. The criticism is that this is a serious limitation on freedom of speech. I have written two or three newspaper articles putting forward this view and various other commentators have made the same argument in the media and at conferences. There has never been, however, any response to these arguments. This is not because there is no one who holds the contrary view. The fact that this kind of legislation exists at the federal and state level indicates that there were powerful groups who persuaded governments to enact those statutes. But those groups obviously feel no need to defend their position or any desire to engage with their opponents in public debate. It is hard to imagine this kind of silence in the US – or even Britain – from one side in a contest about freedom of speech.

It might be said by those organising literary festivals that most of their audiences do not want to be challenged in their views. And there is some truth in that. My observations of audiences over 10 years at the Sydney Writers Festival suggested that most shared the social and political views of the presenters and were not particularly interested in hearing a contrary opinion. That is, however, no reason audiences should not sometimes be confronted with contrary opinions. As I have already suggested, quite apart from the value of public debate, it is simply more fun in my experience to get an argument going on the stage and in the audience. But, as I say, this is not now, if it ever was, part of the Australian tradition.

THE SPECTATOR AUSTRALIA,
21 May 2016

SPEAK UP!

Free speech is struggling in the battle against 'conventional wisdom' and 'political correctness'

It hardly needs saying that freedom of speech, even under the protection of the First Amendment in the United States, has never been an absolute value but has always been subject to a range of qualifications. Everyone is aware of Oliver Wendell Holmes' dictum that no one is at liberty to shout "Fire" in a crowded theatre.

When considering the qualifications to freedom of speech in Australia, the much-discussed section 18C of the federal Racial Discrimination Act is still a useful place to begin because there are somewhat similar provisions – but dealing with a much wider range of community groups – in legislation at the State and Territory level. Section 18C makes it unlawful to do an act that is reasonably likely, in all the circumstances, to offend, insult, humiliate or intimidate another person or a group of people because of the race, colour or national or ethnic origin of the other person or some or all of the persons in the group. There is an exemption in section 18D for anything said or done reasonably and in good faith in a number of situations, including academic and scientific discussions or for "any other genuine purpose in the public interest."

The real complaint about section 18C is that it is not always possible to have a robust public debate without offending or insulting persons or groups with a high level of sensitivity. Yes – there are some exemptions in the legislation but, amongst other problems, it is necessary to show that what was said was said reasonably and in good faith. This can be a highly subjective judgment on the part of a court or tribunal and, in any case, can only occur after the publisher has already been involved in lengthy and costly legal proceedings.

At the State and Territory level, a good example is the Tasmanian Anti-Discrimination Act which prohibits conduct that offends, humiliates, intimidates, insults or ridicules another person on the basis of 14 kinds of status, including marital status, relationship status and family responsibilities. This provision had some publicity in late 2015 when a complaint was made to the Tasmanian Anti-Discrimination Commissioner about a booklet distributed by Church authorities to Catholic school students on the subject of marriage. Presumably it would be open to anyone in Tasmania living in an unmarried heterosexual relationship to make such a complaint as well. Anyone who has read *Brideshead Revisited* will recall that it is Catholic teaching that unmarried heterosexual couples are "living in sin" and doomed to the eternal fires of hell. That sounds like an insult to me!

It is true that, unlike s 18C, the Tasmanian provision has the requirement that a reasonable person would have anticipated that the other person would be offended or insulted. But, putting aside the fact that this is another value judgement for a court or tribunal, it may well be that a publisher does anticipate that some persons will be offended or insulted in the course of a vigorous public debate on moral questions. It is also true that, somewhat similar to s 18C, the Tasmanian legislation has an exception for a public act done in good faith for any purpose in the public interest. But again this can involve highly subjective judgments and requires this defence to be made out affirmatively by a publisher in the course of lengthy and expensive legal proceedings

These kinds of provisions also raise the question of whether there could be a proper public debate in the context of a plebiscite on same-sex marriage or referendum on indigenous recognition in the Constitution. It is easy to imagine some groups in the community being offended by propositions put forward by those arguing a "No" case in any plebiscite or referendum that took place on these issues.

None of this, of course, is to say that incitements to violence against particular groups in the community should not be unlawful. As it happens, they have always been unlawful under the criminal law. But this is very different from expressions of opinion that may be offensive or insulting.

It might be thought that the answer to this and other problems concerning freedom of speech is a bill of rights but that is not a solution. What happens under a bill of rights is that political, social and economic questions are transferred from elected parliamentarians to unelected judges. It is important to realise that political, social and economic questions do not become legal questions when given to a court. They remain what they have always been but they are now decided by a court. Courts in the United States have started with the general proposition that speech under the First Amendment is to be absolutely free and then devised numerous qualifications to that principle. So really nothing has changed except that the qualifications are imposed by courts rather than parliament.

John Kenneth Galbraith coined the phrase the "conventional wisdom" in the 1960s and there has developed in Australia in recent years a conventional wisdom on a whole range of subjects, for example, climate change, boat arrivals, same sex marriage and coal mining to name a few. This consensus is maintained by large sections of the media; all legal professional bodies; most teaching staff in universities; most of those in the senior ranks of the federal and State bureaucracies; and quite a number of the most prominent spokespersons for the business community. Some of these views may be quite supportable. But that is not the point. The point is that no young person in our society could publicly espouse a contrary view if he or she wished to pursue a serious career in any of these areas.

It might be thought that all this is wildly exaggerated. But, there can be little doubt that any young aspiring academic who consistently contradicted the conventional wisdom at morning tea in the staff common room would find his or her career prospects severely affected. And most young academics would know this and would confine their public views accordingly. Much the same position would hold for young persons working in the federal and State bureaucracies and in many large corporations. This is not because everyone in such organisations subscribes to the conventional wisdom but those that do not know better than to expose their views.

There are, of course, strong strains of what is sometimes known as political correctness in England and the United States but, for reasons that are not entirely clear, this development seems to have been taken to extremes in this country. One factor may be that in a much smaller society there is simply less scope for diversity of opinion that in England or the United States.

All of this may sound rather pessimistic when considering the position of freedom of speech in Australia in the immediate future. And it is certainly true that public debate on important political and social questions has become more inhibited in this country over recent years. There are, however, still individuals and journals who are prepared to initiate robust public discussions. They often have a problem getting any response from the smug holders of the conventional wisdom but they can only hope that eventually there will be a reaction against the current claustrophobic climate of opinion.

THE AUSTRALIAN

Friday, June 3, 2016

THE CHURCH OF POLITICAL CORRECTNESS CONTROLS NATIONAL DISCOURSE

Key institutions in Australia are dominated by humourless preachers of PC conformity

The politically correct class in Australia bears many similarities to an evangelical religious movement and it is perhaps no accident that its rise has coincided with a sharp decline in the membership of traditional Protestant church groups. The desire to belong to an organisation with a coherent body of beliefs and to spread this gospel to others has always been a strong one for many people.

Like these older religions the PCC subscribes to a long list of doctrines, some of the most prominent of which are:

- formal legal status for same-sex marriage
- an alarmist view of climate change and its causes
- depiction of Australian society as essentially racist
- support for a bill of rights
- scepticism about the police and other law enforcement agencies, especially in relation to anti-terrorism legislation
- indifference to issues of border security
- hostility to Israel in the context of conflict in the Middle East

It might be noted that none of these views involve any economic costs to those who hold them. The PCC is generally wealthy and concerned to stay that way. Most of its members are not particularly interested in the distribution of society's resources. There is also some overlap between these views and the policies of the Greens, although the PCC generally prefers not to be identified with any particular political party.

Some of these views, of course, may be justifiable in whole or in part, but the PCC is not interested in debating them. Like many religious movements in history, it considers that anyone who rejects even one of these doctrines is not merely misguided but part of an evil conspiracy and deserving of suppression.

The debate over freedom of speech and section 18C of the Racial Discrimination Act exemplified this. By making it unlawful to insult or offend some sections of the community, this provision, if the PCC were to be believed, was necessary to prevent Australians engaging in racist behaviour as bad as in the US deep south in the 1950s and 1960s.

The PCC is relatively small in a numerical sense and many of its tenets are not supported by popular sentiment in the wider community. But its influence is considerable because of where its members are located. This is because its members dominate large sections of the media; most teaching staff in universities; all legal professional bodies; the senior ranks of the federal and state bureaucracies; and the management of several large corporations.

It is not true, of course, that every person in these organisations shares all or even some of the PCC doctrines. But any dissenters would be well aware that their career prospects could be seriously harmed by expressing a contrary opinion. This is particularly true for people at the start of their careers and not yet established in a secure position. And it is again reminiscent of many religious groups: it is not enough to accept most but not all of the doctrines. Disagreement with any one of them leads automatically to exclusion from the group. As in many previous periods of history, silence is often the safest course of action.

There is an interesting question as to how the PCC came to capture so many influential organisations in Australian society, especially since this phenomenon seems to date only from the early 1980s. It is true that there are some strong strains of political correctness in other countries, including Britain and the US, but Australia seems to have led the way in this exercise and produced a much greater stifling of public debate on social and political questions. Why this is so is a conundrum, although the answer may have something to do with the huge expansion of universities over this period and the introduction of PCC material into school curriculum's.

The difficulty about reversing this situation is that once people in organisations realise that a particular set of views is expected of them, they are unlikely to advertise any contrary opinions so the present system is self-reinforcing. There are still contrary voices in Australia to this stifling regime, but any dissenters need to have an established position in society so that they are immune from persecution by these grimly determined and utterly humourless zealots.

THE AUSTRALIAN,

Tuesday, April 4, 2017

SANCTIMONIOUS THOUGHT POLICE TAKING CHARGE OF NATIONAL DEBATES

Too many caving in as manipulative PC brigade seeks a conformity of views

The attempts in recent days by corporations such as Coopers Brewery and public bodies such as Macquarie University to avoid any identification with Christian beliefs is a testament to the powerful regime of political correctness that now operates in Australia. Coopers quickly discovered, to its cost, that there is a big difference between a company that favours same-sex marriage, such as Qantas or PricewaterhouseCoopers, and one that suggests there may be two sides to the debate.

But how has the politically correct class achieved such a high level of control over the public discussion of contestable, social, economic and political questions?

Most people in the bureaucracy, the business sector and the academic community are – quite sensibly – fearful of publicly questioning the conventional wisdom on such issues as levels of immigration, the extent of the terrorist threat, dealing with unauthorised boat arrivals and sources of energy for power generation. Naturally this class is also in favour of section 18C of the Racial Discrimination Act as a protection against what it sees as the inherent racism of most Australians, and a bill of rights that would transfer decisions on many political issues from parliaments to judges, whom they consider better qualified. The recent parliamentary committee report on 18C suggests that many politicians are just as reluctant to speak out on these issues. Some members of the committee apparently favoured changes but were unwilling to be identified by name in the report.

It is true, of course, that some people have been prepared to speak out on these matters but they need to have a relatively secure position - and to be prepared for abuse in much of the media. Opponents of 18C, for example, were described in a *Sydney Morning Herald* editorial as conducting a "campaign to weaken hate speech laws, largely to help media and political insiders to make more money from playing to the base instincts of Australians".

The power of the politically correct class to enforce widespread conformity – at least in public – with its views lies in its control of a range of public and private sector bodies, including:

- most departments and faculties in universities
- many media organisations
- community welfare groups
- professional groups for barristers and solicitors
- literary festivals and writers awards
- governing bodies for commercial sport
- the system for awarding Australian honours
- boards of many government and private sector corporations

These largely interlocking groups are able to exclude from their ranks anyone who expresses controversial opinions, which can be broadly defined as those that contradict or even question the canons of political correctness. It is hardly surprising, therefore, that so many people in these areas choose to adopt a discreet silence when it comes to the discussion of issues with a potential for political discord.

One consequence of this reluctance to take a public position has been the difficulty experienced by the Liberals in securing support for some of their policies from one of their traditional constituencies - the business community. It might be thought that reductions in the corporate tax rate and the scaling back of penalty rates would be strongly supported by private sector bodies. But, in comparison with the vigorous participation of unions in the political process, the activities of those organisations representing business groups have been rather muted, seemingly out of a reluctance to be too closely identified with any political party.

One question that arises from all this is how so many of these bodies were initially captured by the forces of political correctness, given that it is probably only over the last 25 years that this has become such a powerful phenomenon in Australia. There may be some connection with the decline of organised religion, in the sense that some people feel the need for a set of secular pieties to substitute for what were previously religious beliefs. In addition, there has been an explosion of conventional and social media outlets during this period – however, contrary to many expectations, rather than a greater diversity of opinion, this has resulted in increased conformity to conventional views.

Whatever the explanation, many public and private bodies are learning the hard way that the iron rule of political correctness in Australia is not something that can easily be ignored.

THE AUSTRALIAN,
Monday, August 21, 2017

REVISIONISTS DRIVE OLD DIXIE DOWN AGAIN

Warriors of political correctness fight history on the same bloody battlefields

Last week a group of protesters in Durham, North Carolina, tore down a statue of a Confederate soldier which had stood for nearly a century and bore the inscription "In memory of the boys who wore the gray". The violence a few days earlier in Charlottesville, Virginia, had its origins in a dispute over whether a statue of the Confederate general, Robert E Lee, should be removed. All this led the mayor of Baltimore to order that all Confederate statues in the city should be taken down for reasons of public safety.

The notion of the Old South as a lost land of chivalrous cavaliers, fuelled by works like *Gone with the Wind*, was always a myth. It was a society whose economy was largely based on the export of cotton and the harvesting of that crop by slaves. When the Civil War commenced in 1861 it was not fought, as many in the South asserted then and later, over states' rights but over the preservation of slavery. The South feared, probably rightly, that Lincoln's election as president would preclude the extension of slavery outside its current borders and that, in this event, its existence even in the Southern states would come under threat.

But, having said all that, the establishment of the Confederacy and the four years of civil conflict that followed are the most significant events in American history after the revolutionary war that resulted in its separation from Britain in the 1780s. Some of the complexities of the period are illustrated by the fact that Robert E Lee was offered the command of the Union armies but refused when his own state of

Virginia decided to secede from the Union and join the Confederacy. If Lee had taken this command, it is very likely that the war would have been much shorter, given his military skills in comparison to the utterly incompetent generals in charge of the Union forces in the early years of the conflict. All this indicates why it is pointless to try to erase historical events because they do not accord with the views that might be taken about them from a much later period. Yet this is what many practitioners of political correctness aim to do.

At about the same time as the Confederate soldier was being dismantled in North Carolina, the Yarra Council, located – naturally – in some of Melbourne's more affluent suburbs, resolved to remove from its activities any observance of Australia Day on the basis that 26 January 1788 marked an "invasion" of the Australian continent by British forces and so is offensive to indigenous people.

In similar vein there have been complaints over the years in Britain about the statue in London of Sir Arthur Harris who presided over the Allies' bombing campaign against Germany during the Second World War, despite the fact that more than 40,000 civilians were killed by German bombing over England during the same period and at least three times as many suffered injury.

The forces of political correctness in all these countries are prepared to wage a war on much of modern history because they believe that anything, past or present, that is inconsistent with their fiercely-held articles of faith must be expunged. These zealous beliefs include:

- hostility to all forms of Christian religion but especially the Catholic church;
- suspicion of the activities of law enforcement bodies, particularly in the area of anti-terrorism but in the criminal law generally;
- a sentiment in favour of open borders and so against

any restrictions on refugees, whether economic or otherwise, entering the country;

- an alarmist view of climate change and its causes;
- support for transferring political questions from parliaments to courts by way of a bill of rights;
- preference for rule by international bodies, such as the UN or the European Community, over national governments, including the Australian government.

It might be noted that none of these views involve the members of the political correct class, who are invariably well-off, in making any financial or other sacrifices in the course of their crusades.

The antipathy to inconvenient historical facts is also reflected in the so-called "trigger warnings" that have been instituted in quite a number of American universities and in some Australian universities. These are particularly relevant to history courses because it is especially in these studies that some highly sensitive students might encounter material that they find offensive. They must, therefore, be warned in advance of the offensive material lest their delicate feelings be injured. History is just another battlefield for the warriors of political correctness.

THE SPECTATOR AUSTRALIA

21 April 2018

SORRY SEEMS TO BE THE EASIEST WORD

I am sorry to have to say this but I think we all need a break from apologies.

When I was practising in media law at the Bar one of the most common forms of apology by publishers, confronted with an unwinnable defamation action, was in the following form:

> Some readers may have taken our recent article as suggesting that the Minister was corrupt. We did not intend to make any such suggestion and apologise for any hurt or embarrassment caused to the Minister by this publication.

The publisher had, of course, absolutely intended to say that the Minister was corrupt and was only apologising as part of a legal settlement that may also have involved the payment of damages. The avalanche of public apologies over recent years in many areas has a similar element of meaninglessness.

There may be a real question about what penalty Australia's ball-tampering cricketers deserved, given the way this conduct by players from other countries has been treated in the past, but the one pointless aspect of their press conferences was their series of tearful apologies. The ball-tampering was planned in advance and no doubt their real regret is that it was obvious on the television coverage of the match.

For a politically correct apology, however, it is hard to beat the performance last month of the editor-in-chief of *National Geographic*, Susan Goldberg, who referred to the magazine's "appalling" coverage of different races and nationalities over its 130 year existence. One item singled out by Goldberg was a 1930 article describing the crowning of Haile Selassie as emperor of Ethiopia! For a totally insincere apology, on the other hand, the prize might go to Bill Clinton who said of his encounter – affair is hardly the right word – with Monica Lewinsky: "I misled people, including even my wife. I deeply regret that." As for the apology that ignores reality, one of the best examples was that issued by Uruguayan soccer player Luis Suarez after he had bitten Italy's Giorgio Chiellini at the World Cup in 2014. According to Surez, Chiellini "suffered the physical result of a bite in the collision he suffered with me." It will be observed in this statement there seems to be no positive action of any kind on Surez's part.

The Prime Minister is said to be considering an apology – on behalf of the nation – to those persons identified as victims by the royal commission into institutional responses to child sexual abuse. These persons are quite rightly the subject of great sympathy in the community but the fact is the abuse was carried out by a relatively small group of individuals in positions of authority in public and private institutions over the post-war years. The vast majority of Australians then and now have never contemplated this kind of conduct and there is something puzzling about an apology that suggests that they were in some way responsible for what happened in those institutions.

The cult of the apology has been extended to events in modern history but why stop there? Should not the descendants of the Normans, if any can be traced now, apologise for their behaviour towards the Saxons after the invasion by William the Conqueror? And, what about the descendants of the Vikings for their centuries of murder and pillage along the English coastline? In this spirit Pope John Paul II apologised in 1992 for the church's condemnation of Galileo in 1633. Galileo's offence was to claim that the earth revolved around the sun and he came very close to being burnt at the stake. He retracted his claim but still spent the rest of his life closely confined to his own quarters.

It might be argued, however, that there are genuine cases of collective guilt in the modern era. The Germans, for example, largely welcomed the Hitler regime in the 1930s and could hardly avoid knowing about its policies of extermination in much of occupied Europe. But what is the worth of an apology from a later German government to someone whose family perished in the death camps? If some conduct, like ball-tampering, is too trivial for an apology, some crimes are too great for any expression of regret. So too are some blunders. Robert McNamara confessed in his 1995 memoir that he was mistaken in his – highly successful – efforts as Secretary of Defence in the Kennedy and Johnson administrations to bring about large-scale American involvement in the Vietnam War – an involvement that resulted in 525,000 US troops being in Vietnam by mid 1967. Small comfort, perhaps for the 55,000 Americans and 500 Australians who lost their lives in the conflict.

There is a ritualistic quality to so many of the apologies that are published almost every day in the media, from politicians who are sorry for what their extra-marital affairs have done to their families, to footballers who express remorse for the damage done to their club's reputation by their night-club brawling.

There is a place for apologies in the personal relationships of individuals. For this kind of apology it is hard to go past the letter written by Abraham Lincoln to General Ulysses S Grant in July 1863. Lincoln had doubted one of Grant's decisions in the middle of the Civil War but, when Grant won a great victory, Lincoln wrote to congratulate him and added: "I feared it was a mistake, I now wish to make the personal acknowledgement that you were right and I was wrong."

This was a private communication by Lincoln but in recent times the public apology has become a tedious piece of theatre that we could well do without. The best advice on this subject may have come from P G Wodehouse: "It is a good rule in life never to apologise. The right sort of people do not want apologies, and the wrong sort take a mean advantage of them."

THE AUSTRALIAN,

Monday, June 18, 2018

DON'T DARE SPEAK IF YOU THINK FOR YOURSELF

Australia's politically correct brigade is not interested in the truth – too often it hurts

The politically correct class in Australia have always been particularly zealous in their defence of provisions like section 18C of the federal Racial Discrimination Act and similar provisions in the anti-discrimination laws of the States and Territories. These statutes make it unlawful to publish material that, in many cases, does no more than offend the susceptibilities of various groups in the community. What these laws do is to place a higher value on hurt feelings than on the rigorous public debate of political, social and economic questions.

It is under one of those laws that Channel Nine and Sonia Kruger are facing legal proceedings alleging racial vilification. In a morning television program Kruger attempted to discuss the question of whether there was any correlation between Muslim immigration and terrorist incidents in different countries.

When it comes to their own participation in public debate, however, the politically correct class often has few limits on offensive and insulting statements. When two members of the Senate proposed the amendment of section 18C in 2016 they were described by the chief political correspondent of the *Sydney Morning Herald* as "hate-speech apologists". In addition one was said to be "a boorish, supercilious know-all with the empathy of a Besser block" and the other "an absurdist fringe-dweller". Both were "self-promoting misanthropes". At about the same time in a *Herald* cartoon of the prime minister speaking about refugees at the UN he was shown as wearing three badges inscribed with: 'Hate makes the world go around', 'Hate will find a way', and 'All you need is hate'.

More recently there were the comments of a history professor at Sydney University who asked whether *The Australian's* Greg Sheridan and Chris Kenny "think that Western countries are succumbing to a poisonous cocktail of multiculturalism, Muslim immigration, political correctness and cultural Marxism" and added "It seems that, much like Anders Breivik and Steve Bannon they do". Putting aside this categorisation of Bannon, Breivik was the person who killed seventy-seven people on one day in Norway in July 2011. This material was published in, of all places, the ABC's religion and ethics website but the reference to Breivik was later removed by the ABC. The professor said "I think some people have overreached themselves with their incendiary rhetoric". Quite so!

Sydney University staff have no monopoly on inflammatory statements. An edition of the student newspaper in May carried the photo on the cover of a female suicide bomber who had killed dozens of Israeli soldiers, describing her as a "martyr" in the struggle against "Israeli colonisation". When the Australian Union of Jewish Students complained about this, the student representative council passed a motion condemning them and congratulating those who had worked on the newspaper "for their brave and highly defensible cover depicting a pro-Palestine freedom fighter".

The domination of universities in Australia by the politically correct class is, of course, not a recent phenomenon. But their influence is just as pervasive in most public institutions and many private ones, including the boards of many public companies who often seem to be more concerned with taking a political stance than making a profit for their shareholders. What is interesting, however, is the contrast between this group's view of themselves as the moral guardians of society and their ferocious intolerance for anyone who expresses a view contrary to their own. It is as if those contrary views represent a threat to their role of moral guardians whereas they occupy most of the commanding heights of Australian society and are unfortunately not at all threatened. One thing they have done, however, is to lower the tone of public debate by virulent attacks on their opponents that reflect the deep intensity of their sanctimonious opinions.

ROYALS AND REPUBLICANS

I have never shared the affection that even some republicans seem to have for the House of Windsor and I had always assumed that they could be removed from Australia's system of government by substituting for the Governor General a president chosen by a majority of the federal parliament sufficient to prevent the government of the day having the sole choice on this question.

But the determination of many republicans to have a popularly elected president caused the failure of the 1999 referendum and continuing division on this issue has significantly diminished the prospects of achieving a republic in the immediate future. There are many supporters of the concept of a republic who nevertheless see an elected president as becoming a counterpoint to the Prime Minister and a destabilising element in Australian politics.

ROYALS AND REPUBLICANS

THE SYDNEY MORNING HERALD

Saturday, March 2, 1985

THE WORLD'S GREATEST SOAP OPERA

Matriarch: Queen Mary and the House of Windsor by Anne Edwards

This is a book of appalling style and yet quite interesting content. The author's previous works include biographies of Margaret Mitchell (author of *Gone With The Wind*), Vivien Leigh and Judy Garland. This is hardly promising but she is obviously a student of soap opera and there is no longer running soap opera than the House of Windsor.

The cloying schoolgirl style can be illustrated by the following passage relating to the Jubilee celebrations of 1935 for George V and Queen Mary:

> Queen Mary knew her husband was dying and that her days as Queen Consort were numbered. Would the King have lived longer without the physical exhaustion the Jubilee was to cost him? Perhaps, but the nation's enthusiasm did give him great happiness.

Despite the total absence of analytical skills, the author has collected an extraordinary mass of information about the House of Windsor. That is obviously a valuable, if possibly unconscious, political exercise in itself.

The book's subject was born in 1867 as the daughter of the Duke and Duchess of Teck – a minor German principality. She grew up in Kensington Palace in London in the court of Queen Victoria and was selected in 1892 to wed Prince Eddy, the eldest son of the then Prince of Wales (later Edward VII). Prince Eddy, who was both physically and mentally retarded, died that same year. Various rumours surrounded his death, including one that he was the real Jack the Ripper, and another that he was poisoned by the Royal family so that he could never embarrass them by assuming the throne.

It is remarkable that, right down to the present day, the House of Windsor has produced so many persons, of below-average physical and mental qualities. One reason for this is undoubtedly the extensive in-breeding that has taken place over the past two centuries in European royalty in general and the House of Windsor in particular. The present Queen Elizabeth II and prince Philip are cousins, as were Queen Mary and George V. The palace bureaucracy had been quite happy to see Mary wed to Prince Eddy despite his retarded condition. When he died they were equally happy to see her passed on to his younger brother, George. So she entered the House of Windsor, or the House of Saxe-Coburg-Gotha, as it was until the 1914-18 war prompted the change from the German.

Her father-in-law became King Edward VII in 1901 at the age of 59. His chief amusements were stuffing the pockets of his guests' dinner jackets with sticky sweets and squirting them with bicycle pumps filled with water. Her husband, who became King George V in 1910, relaxed by shooting 4,000 pheasants in a day on his estates at Sandringham after they had been flushed out by 100 beaters. George V's eldest son was Edward VIII, who succeeded to the throne in 1936 and abdicated the same year to marry Mrs Simpson. He was succeeded by George VI, his stuttering and dipsomaniac brother. Queen Mary outlived all these and died in 1953, by which time her grand-daughter Elizabeth II, was on the throne. She never forgave her eldest son for giving up his crown and remained hostile to him to the end.

The relentless accumulation of information by the author provides the basis for the present condition of the House of Windsor. There was an earlier tradition of ensuring that the children had no education whatsoever. In many cases, including the children of George V and Queen Mary, the isolated and oppressive experience of childhood produced conditions that could never be rectified in later life. The overall result has been an extended family that, even with the colossal wealth and resources available to it, has never produced a single person of any genuine intellectual artistic or sporting capacity. The only activity to which its members have ever been inspired is that of the preserving their own political position. Few of them have ever displayed the slightest interest in any other economic or social issues.

It is hardly surprising in this context that the House of Windsor's political preferences emerge from the book as conservative. The role of George V in the formation of the National Government in Britain in 1931 was a dramatic example of this preference. That episode should also dispel the myth that a constitutional monarch does not have opportunities for the exercise of political power.

But such incidents are aside to the real issue. The classic objection to monarchy as an element of government is its inconsistency with democratic political theory. This objection is, of course, impossible to overcome. What this book demonstrates, however – no doubt much against the author's wishes – is that even apart from political theory, it is insulting to have such a talentless and unattractive family as the constitutional rulers of Australia.

THE SYDNEY MORNING HERALD

Saturday, April 1, 2000

NO FAIRYTALE ENDINGS IN SPENCER FAMILY SAGA

Diana and the Rise of the House of Spencer by Anne Edwards

The Spencer Family by Charles Spencer

Both these books, either in whole or in part, recount the story of the union between two of Britain's great dysfunctional families – the Windsors and the Spencers. This was like one of the Simpsons marrying into the Addams family – with predictable results.

Anne Edwards has written half a dozen biographies, chiefly of royalty and film stars. Her style is often a little breathless, but she has collected a wealth of detail about the life and times of Diana Spencer. Much of the information may have been published in other sources, but not in an organised and chronological fashion. There have been biographies of Charles – by Jonathan Dimbleby – and of Diana – by Andrew Morton – but these were essentially works by advocates in the context of divorce proceedings.

Diana seems to have had an unhappy childhood, spent mostly at boarding schools after her parents' bitter split and the appearance of a hated stepmother. She was unable to pass even the most basic exams, but seems to have had a determined personality. When her eldest sister's attempts to marry Charles failed, she took up the challenge. The timing was right. By the late 1970s the Queen and other members of the royal family were determined that the future king should have a picture-postcard family. The author alleges that there was an official short list of prospective brides, initially drawn up by the palace and then refined by Charles's two chief mistresses – Camilla Parker Bowles and the Australian Dale Tryon.

The future was clear from the honeymoon on the royal yacht. Diana threw up after every meal and the royal psychiatrists were waiting when the boat returned. She found the Windsors tasteless and boring with only one agenda – the preservation of their existing position and entitlements. The sheer scope of these entitlements emerges dramatically from the book's accounts of life at the various palaces and of the constant vacations in exotic locations. Servants and retainers are legion and no royal whim is left unsatisfied by taxpayers' resources.

Despite the birth of two children, the marriage did not improve. Diana's bulimia continued and there were several wrist-slashings. Parker Bowles became an obsession with Diana, who seemed bewildered that her rival was older and, at least in conventional terms, not as beautiful. As it happened, Parker Bowles looked like what she was – a quite attractive woman, rather closer to Charles's age and interests.

The author gives many examples of how the marriage had become one of intense passion – not of love but of hatred. In 1987, for example, Charles and Diana spent five weeks of the year living under the same roof. These are also the years of Diana's affairs, particularly with Captain James Hewitt. There were many people, including journalists, who were aware of the reality but, as in the case of King Edward and Mrs Simpson, most public references were heavily sanitised. When the gloves finally came off, each side leaked damaging material to the press. There was plenty of this to go round, with the low point perhaps being the infantile telephone sex tapes between Charles and Parker Bowles and between Diana and someone called "Squidgy". This all culminated in the two poisonous television interviews where both combatants put their case to the public.

The divorce left Diana with £15 million ($40 million) and the world's most famous face. The book gives a graphic description of the last few years with the world as her stage and a constantly changing cast of romantic leads, ranging from captain of the English rugby team to, finally, the social-climbing playboy. Some commentators have tried to find some public significance in Diana's life and death, but the reality is that, at the end of it all, she was just a pretty face.

The history of the Spencer family – by Diana's brother, the current Earl – is unfortunately much less entertaining than Edwards's biography. The first Earl was given his title by Charles I during the Civil War. The family has always been enormously wealthy and was a bastion of the Whig party in the 18th and 19th centuries. Its most famous member – before Diana, of course – was Georgiana, Duchess of Devonshire and the model for Lady Teazle in Sheridan's *School for Scandal.* Most members of the family appear, however, to have been rather dull and the record of their expenditures on horses and foxhounds soon pall. The Spencers always hoped to marry into the royal family, but presumably not in the way this finally occurred. The book is a useful historical record and the illustrations are sumptuous, with many portraits reproduced in glossy colour.

There is a wonderful scene as described in Edwards's book but, perhaps not surprisingly, omitted from the official family history – where the current Earl, who came into £76 million on his father's death, searches his stepmother's bags after the funeral having ordered her from the house in order to make sure she has not packed any of the silverware.

All this might suggest that the result in last November's republic referendum was bizarre. But the truth is that a large majority of the electorate has long been prepared to vote for severing Australian constitutional ties with the British monarchy. Instead, however, the campaign went off on a debate about the role of a president. If the right question is ever put, copies of these books could be left in the polling booths to make the result absolutely certain.

THE AUSTRALIAN

Friday, January 29, 2016

JUST WHAT KIND OF PRESIDENT WOULD WE WANT

Republicans need to make their aims clear before they can get anywhere

In 1967 I was one of the foundation members of the Melbourne University Republican Club. There was an inaugural meeting but there didn't seem to be anything that we could usefully do at that time and we never met again. This is perhaps indicative of the sad history of the republican movement in Australia.

As everyone is aware, the 1999 referendum was lost because of divisions amongst republicans as to whether a president should be appointed by the parliament or elected by popular vote. One of the puzzles about the republican campaign was the endless slogan that a change was necessary so that an Australian could be the country's head of state. There is a good argument that there is no need for a head of state at all. The US president is both head of state and head of government. Australia has a prime minister who is head of government and could certainly carry out both roles. Countries like Ireland and Germany have a president but this is essentially a ceremonial role like that of the governor general in this country.

Even assuming, however, that a republican model in Australia would include a ceremonial president, the obvious reason to support a change to a republic is to break the link with the British monarchy and there are three reasons why that should happen. The first is that it is the monarchy of another country, although this is not to denigrate in any way the enormous British legacy to Australia in the form of its legal and political regimes. The second reason is that the monarchy is by definition an hereditary institution and so fundamentally inconsistent with the concept of democracy. The third reason is that the history of the Windsors over the last century is far from inspiring and has not really been changed by the constant public relations exercises over recent years centered on some of the younger members of the family.

Arguably it has always been a mistake for the Australian republican campaign to extol the virtues of the present Queen and say that its campaign is no reflection on her. This is sending a mixed message to the electorate. If the Queen is so wonderful, why is there any need for a change? This schizophrenic position has led some republicans to the bizarre proposition that nothing should occur as long as the Queen remains on the throne, as if significant political questions were to be determined by the personality of the monarch and not the nature of the monarchy.

All this still leaves as a question for republicans how any president under a new system would be chosen. Even if it is assumed that the powers of a president would be the same as those exercised by the governor general, there can be little doubt that a president elected by popular vote would have a very different role from one appointed by the parliament. There would be an almost irresistible temptation for such an office-holder to set himself or herself up as a counterpoint to the prime minister and to take up issues that the government would not, for whatever reason, be prepared to espouse. It is hard to see the point of introducing this kind of destabilising element into the current political system where a government and a prime minister are elected to decide on the political agenda between elections.

There are, however, plenty of people on the republican side who want to destabilise the current political system. In addition to the desire for an activist president, there are those who want to change the Constitution to introduce a bill of rights, to abolish the States or to deal with the status of indigenous members of the community. All of these are subjects for legitimate political debate but any of them would derail a plebiscite or referendum on a republic because these are all issues on which there are significant divisions of opinion within the electorate.

The prospects for a national vote on the republic question seem slight in the immediate future. If there were to be a vote and the choice is between a member of the House of Windsor and a popularly-elected game show host, even life-long republicans like myself may find this a difficult choice.

THE SPECTATOR AUSTRALIA

9 June 2018

ON REPUBLICANISM

The spectacle of so many grisly celebrities clustered together at the royal wedding reminded me of why I was once a fervent republican.

When I joined the Melbourne University Republican Club in 1967 as a founding member, I must confess that my colleagues and myself had not given a lot of thought to the issue of a republic. I suspect we were largely motivated to remove the Windsors from the Australian system of government. There were two reasons for this concern. The first was an objection to the notion of an hereditary monarchy, although even those of Irish decent in what was then a totally Anglo-Celtic group appreciated the enormous legacy of the Westminster system of government that Australia had taken from Britain. The second reason was that the Windsors seemed such a tasteless and talentless group who had nothing to offer the Australia of the post-war years.

Fifty years on there are a lot more Windsors and they are now international celebrities along the lines of Hollywood movie stars and sporting icons. So perhaps it was hardly surprising that many of guests at the royal wedding were fellow celebrities who were presumably scarcely known to the bride and groom.

But this development underlines the fact that the republican movement in Australia has never been prepared to make the Windsors themselves a political issue. Most republicans over the years have stressed what a wonderful person Queen Elizabeth is and what a marvellous job she is doing. If this is correct, members of the general community could be forgiven for thinking that there is little point in changing the existing situation. Similarly, a number of prominent republicans suggested they were looking forward to the royal wedding and hoped everyone would enjoy it as much as they did.

The most consistent slogan of the republican movement has been the importance of having an Australian as our 'head of state' – with the object of ensuring that every Australian child would have the opportunity to become that head of state. This question is uncertain at the outset because there is a reasonable legal argument that the Governor-General and not the Queen is Australia's head of state. But, putting that to one side, it might be thought that the real issue is that the Queen is the sovereign at the apex of Australia's system of government. Again, however, the republican movement has tried to avoid focusing on the role of the Queen and has only succeeded in confusing the issue.

Another assumption that I think we made in 1967 was that an Australian president, who might still be called the Governor-General under a republican model, would be chosen by the government of the day in the same way that the Governor-General has been chosen in the post-war years. The idea of a popular vote for the presidency, with game show hosts and movie stars vying with each other, would never have occurred to us. But this is now a real possibility if a republican model were ever to be adopted. Quite apart from the trivial candidates that might be attracted by this exercise, there is an important objection by way of public administration to a directly-elected president who would then be in a position to set himself or herself up as a rival to the prime minister in the eyes of the general community.

In many ways, of course, Australia is very much a republic rather than a constitutional monarchy of the kind found in Britain and several other European countries. This is because the Queen has absolutely no practical participation in any aspect of Australian government. This was graphically demonstrated in November 1975 when Sir John Kerr removed the Whitlam government, although the

Queen could not have done so and had no role in the confrontation between the Senate and the government.

There was some debate at the time of the republic referendum in 1999 as to whether the so-called reserve powers, originally derived from the sovereign but exercised in Australia by the Governor General, could be codified and at the same time cut back. This has effectively occurred in, for example, New South Wales where the introduction of fixed term parliaments and their requirement of a successful motion of no confidence in the government before an early election can be called has limited some of the Governor's previous reserve powers. But it must be remembered that the NSW Legislative Council cannot block a government's budget in the way the Senate did in 1975. As long as the Senate retains this power under the federal Constitution it will always be theoretically possible to have a repeat of the events of November 1975.

One particular problem for the republican movement is that, if the question of constitutional change is revisited at some time in the future, there will likely to be proposals for other and even more controversial changes, such as the introduction of a bill of rights or the abolition of the States, on the basis that, if there is to be a referendum, a whole series of amendments to the Constitution can be put to the electorate at the same time. If the issue of a republic becomes confused with these kinds of issues, its prospects of success would almost certainly be significantly diminished.

So where to from here for the idea of a republic? It must be said that the political landscape is far from promising. My own youthful fervour has somewhat declined with the prospect of an elected president emerging from any future adoption of a republican model, although my aversion to the House of Windsor has not diminished. As for the Melbourne University republican club, it never met again after its inaugural assembly. We couldn't think of any action to take to advance the cause of a republic and, in many ways, that is still the problem for the republican movement today.

AUSTRALIAN POLITICS

It was often said that the Whitlam government was in office but not in power but, to some extent, the electoral domination of the Liberals since 1996 raises the same question. A number of these pieces suggest that the ability of any federal government to confine its functions or to limit its expenditures is severely constrained by the expectations of the Australian electorate. In the case of the Liberals, their capacity to influence the currents of society is also limited, in this case by their loss of control over many centres of influence in both the public and private sectors.

The problems of government in Australia are accentuated by the Senate where it is now almost impossible for either of the major parties to obtain a majority and the cross-benchers, particularly the Greens, provide a degree of instability for any administration.

It might be thought that the Liberals' victories at the national level and in New South Wales in 2019 demonstrate their electoral strength but both results were gained by the narrowest of margins and do not alter the reality of how their opponents have effectively captured much of the political agenda.

AUSTRALIAN POLITICS

THE BULLETIN

October 23, 1984

WHY THE LIBS CAN'T FILL MENZIES' BOOTS

In many ways it is the election set down for December 1 – rather than the election of March 1983 – that represents the end of a remarkable period of domination of federal politics by the Liberal and National parties.

For the last time since 1946 the two parties are going into an election campaign knowing that – in the absence of a miracle – they cannot win. Despite some real fears before the 1983 campaign, there was no such feeling of certainty about its result when the election was called.

In the 35 years since Robert Menzies' victory in 1949 the coalition parties have spent 30 years in office and during the three years of the Whitlam government they quite successfully refused to acknowledge the legitimacy of the new administration. Throughout the period of that government, they always remained on the verge of returning to power through the mechanism of blocking supply in the Senate and forcing an election.

Only in the past 18 months have they experienced the kind of arid opposition in which the Labor Party spent decades in the post-war years.

This era of political dominance produced two great illusions which have not been totally dissipated by those past 18 months in opposition.

The first is that the coalition, particularly the Liberal Party – the most prominent member – as the natural party of government. This is how the Liberals appeared throughout the 50s, 60 and 70s – and not only to themselves but also to most of their opponents and to the electorate at large.

Yet, for most of the 50s and 60s, their dominance was the result of three essentially unrelated factors – the continued growth of the post-war economy, the prominence of foreign affairs as an election issue and the great split within the Labor Party that produced the Democratic Labor Party (DLP).

The political benefits of economic growth flowed naturally to the Liberals as the incumbents from the start of the period of post-war prosperity. By the early 70s it was clear that the economic machine had slowed permanently and that no future government would be able to bask in the aura of affluence that surrounded the Menzies Administration.

The second factor in liberal ascendancy – the role of foreign affairs an as election issue – had already lost much of its potency by the 1969 election. It was perhaps Whitlam's most effective exercise in Opposition to defuse foreign affairs as an item on the political agenda after the damage done to Labor by Menzies' use of the issue at all the elections that he won. And there would appear to be little risk that this issue could become an electoral problem for Labor under a Hawke government.

The consequences of the split lingered until 1974 when the DLP was finally wiped out as a parliamentary group in the Senate. Its rationale had, however, been effectively destroyed by the election of the Whitlam government. The Whitlam government did not last but the DLP never reappeared as a political force.

In retrospect it can be seen how fortuitous was the combination of factors that preserved Liberal rule throughout these decades. This, of course, made the results no less devastating for the Labor Party and helped to produce the debacle of the Whitlam government by ensuring that none of its ministers had previously held office and that many of them were burnt-out cases after so many years of opposition.

Yet some Liberals seem to believe that these halcyon days can be recaptured. They cannot. Quite clearly, the Liberals eventually will return to office in Canberra but not as the natural party of government in the sense that they appeared to be between 1949 and 1983.

The other great illusion about this period of Liberal rule is that it was based upon principles of free enterprise and small government and that these philosophies hold the key to returning to power.

Very few Liberals would hold this view of the Fraser years, presumably. The Valder report, which resulted from a study by senior Liberals of the 1983 election loss, was particularly caustic concerning the failure of that government to live up to its incoming rhetoric of reducing the public sector and deregulating the private sector. But it requires a very short memory to suggest that the Menzies government and its immediate successors were different in this respect from the Fraser regime.

The 50s and 60s were the period when the strongly regulated and anti-competitive structure of the Australian economy was established. Tariff barriers were set in the manufacturing area that produced totally inefficient sectors such as the car industry. The two-airline policy was enshrined in legislation and the importation of aircraft prohibited to ensure that no new service could be established. Banking licences were frozen in the hands of existing holders and the establishment of foreign banks prohibited. Interest rates were tightly regulated and the rates for home loans fixed at an artificially low level. Broadcasting and television licences were issued to existing media outlets and the issue of additional licences or the transference of existing licences closely regulated. A policy of central wage-fixing by the Conciliation and Arbitration Commission was encouraged by the government and adopted as far as possible by the commission under Sir Richard Kirby.

Whether the kind of free market models recommended by the Valder report have any utility for the Australian economy at this stage is not an issue for debate in this article, although it might be argued that – whatever their initial merits – it would be extremely difficult to impose these models on an economy that is the result of the policies described and pursued over decades by Liberal governments.

What is a matter for debate is the assumption in the Valder report that free market policies will be electorally appealing. The Liberal successes of the post-war years were not the result of free market rhetoric or, as can be seen from the list above, free market practice. In addition to preserving this illusion, the rhetoric of the Valder report involves the potential embarrassment for the Liberals of yet again making promises that cannot be performed. As Malcolm Fraser discovered, the realities of power do not allow a great deal of room for manoeuvre in government in this country. It is difficult to make major changes at either the economic or the social level. The Hawke government has been making the same discovery. Its attempts to make two relatively minor changes in the tax and social security areas – the lump sum superannuation tax and the assets test for pensioners – met with ferocious resistance from the groups affected and eventually forced the abandonment of the changes as originally proposed by the government.

In light of these experiences, the kinds of policies suggested by the Valder report are simply exercises in fantasy or, in words previously more appropriate to some sections of the Labor Party, the politics of the warm inner glow.

None of this means that the Liberals do not have some prospects of regaining office in 1987, although this would be a very difficult task if they gained no ground – or even lost ground – in the forthcoming election. But they are not likely to be helped to this end by documents such as the Valder report.

In looking at the post-war period, there is some argument for saying that the Labor Party is not so disconcerted by the concept of opposition as are the Liberals. A cynic might remark that this is hardly surprising at the national level because Labor has had so much more experience in the role. But there is another reason. In many ways the Labor Party more closely resembles the moderate left and centre parties of western Europe with their detailed platforms and their parliamentary membership of long-term politicians who expect to spend some periods out of government. Francois Mitterrand came to the presidency in France, for example, after almost 30 years in continuous opposition and after creating both a set of policies and an administrative structure for the French Socialist Party.

The comparisons cannot be pushed too far but the Liberal Party bears a closer resemblance to the two major parties in the United States. Both the Republicans and Democrats are less parties of detailed policies and complex administrative structures than loose organisations that focus primarily on elections at regular intervals. During periods of government, this structure is highly convenient and unobtrusive but it is more difficult to mobilise in opposition than is the Labor Party's more elaborate machinery.

None of this is much present consolation to Liberals or to their beleaguered leader Andrew Peacock. Peacock represents in some respects a last link, despite his relative youth, with the golden age of Menzies. He succeeded Menzies in the electorate of Kooyong as was looked upon even then as a future prime minister. Except for Fraser, the Liberal leaders since Menzies have struggled badly. It is unfair to put Peacock in the same category as Holt, Snedden, Gorton and McMahon because he is much better.

But it is quite possible that in the aftermath of the forthcoming election, with the long-held confidence of being born to rule at last shattered, the Liberals will reject this link also with their glorious years.

Whatever happens to Peacock, when the Liberals on December 2 confront the prospect of opposition until 1987 – and possibly until 1990 – they will be in no doubt that the past, real or imaginary cannot be recaptured.

THE AUSTRALIAN

Thursday, September 30, 2010

MORE SCRUTINY OF GREENS WILL CURB THEIR INFLUENCE

The party's electoral threat to Labor is real, but its ideas will eventually be discredited

What is to be made of the vote for the Australian Greens on August 21? They polled almost 11.5 per cent of the national vote for the House of Representatives – although spread very unevenly across those 150 seats – and almost 13 per cent of the Senate total.

Some of these votes no doubt represent a protest against the long-established domination of the Australian political system by the two major parties (counting the Liberals and Nationals as one group for these purposes). For 25 years from the late 1970s the Australian Democrats received at least some of their support on this basis. It may be recalled that in the 1977 election they polled almost 10 per cent of the House of Representatives vote and 11 per cent of the Senate vote.

Another factor in support for the Greens is the obvious attractiveness of their stated goals. Who is not, at least theoretically, in favour of sustainable development, cleaner air, more public transport, the preservation of the Great Barrier Reef and the conversation of scarce water resources? There may be difficult questions about the costs of some of these exercises but those problems are seldom referred to by the Greens. Oddly enough, little is ever heard from the Greens on the question of population, which could be considered the most important starting point on issues of sustainability.

The most interesting question in all of this is what proportion of those who voted for the Green on August 21 would endorse the underlying views shared by most of the activists who administer the party, these include:

- a deep suspicion of economic development in general and of the activities of the mining industry and some commercial agriculture in particular.
- opposition to Australian participation in Afghanistan.
- hostility to the police and other law enforcement agencies, especially in relation to anti-terrorism legislation.
- indifference to issues of border security.
- antipathy to the role of the United States in world affairs and most particularly to its support for Israel in the conflict in the Middle East.

It should be obvious that none of these views are held by the two main parties, or presumably by most of those who cast their primary votes for them. It would, however, be unrealistic to assume that these opinions are not shared by some proportion of Green voters, particularly in those inner-city areas in Melbourne and Sydney where Greens' support reached its high-water mark.

Nor should it be assumed that these views are unfashionable. On the contrary, they are strongly held by significant sections of the media, academe, the union movement, the churches and the legal profession. These groups may not generally vote for the Greens – at least so far – but they are in fact much closer to them ideologically than they are to either of the two major parties. It does not matter, however, that these groups do not vote for the Greens. Their significance lies not in their numbers – which are quite small – but in the positions they hold and the influence they wield.

In many ways the Greens are a classic example of what Marx

would have described as a bourgeois party. They reflect the interest of their members and core voters who are consumers rather than producers in the Australian economy, and they do so under the guise of speaking out for the less privileged members of society.

So, where do the Greens go from here? Their new role as holders of the balance of power in the Senate will mean lengthy negotiations with the bigger parties and – almost certainly – compromises with some of their existing positions. This more public role may lead to their sharing in some of the disenchantment that part of the electorate always seems to feel towards the main parties, although there is no other obvious group at present that might be the beneficiary of this disenchantment other than the Greens. It also may lead to divisions within the Greens, both at the parliamentary level and amongst party members, depending on the degree of any compromises.

In one sense, of course, the Greens pose a much greater threat to Labor than to the Coalition, because any beachheads made at the lower house level, including the forthcoming Victorian election in November and the NSW election in March of next year, would almost certainly be at the expense of Labor candidates. On the other hand, it can be expected that any Greens elected to a lower house would support a Labor government at present if that was the difference between Labor forming government or not.

The history of third parties in Australian politics is fairly bleak. None have survived in the long term. The Democratic Labor Party had an effective life of almost 20 years and the Australian Democrats just over 25 years. The fact that the Greens are well outside the mainstream of current political debate in Australia is both a strength and a weakness. It guarantees a certain cohesion amongst party members and core voters but greater public exposure of their true character is likely to cause wariness in the electorate over a longer period of time.

THE AUSTRALIAN

Thursday, November 18 2010

NON-POLITICIANS DON'T HOLD KEY TO ELYSIAN WORLD

Tough decisions would not fare better in the hands of politically platonic guardians

In the aftermath of Australia's August election and the US mid-term poll, there has been another explosion of that age-old phenomenon – the anti-politics movement.

This can best be described as the theory that, if only persons of good will could be unleashed on economic and social problems, these difficulties could be quickly solved – but the partisan conduct of political parties and the selfishness of interest groups in the community prevents this happening. On occasions, of course, governments, although themselves the arm of a political party, put forward this fantasy. They argue that opponents of their policies are acting out of self-interest – as if most of them would be acting out of anything else. They may even accuse the opposition parties of playing politics – as if they would not be carrying out their constitutional role.

The truth is that many political decisions involve hard choices about the allocation of scarce resources. There is, for example, not enough water to go around in the Murray-Darling Basin and someone is going to have to decide how much is going to go to the various competing groups. Similarly, there is considerable agreement on the goal of cutting greenhouse emissions but this will be an expensive process. There will have to be a decision as to who pays for this exercise, including the impact on power bills for individual households. And in the case of roads, there is a real question whether tolls on motorists should be used not only to cover the cost of new freeways but also to subsidise public transport users.

Consulting committees of experts on these questions or holding community forums to discuss them does not make the ultimate decision any less a political one – or any less difficult. One of the fallacies in the case for a Bill of Rights is that it is possible to take political issues – like freedom of speech or freedom of association – and turn them into legal questions by handing them over to courts. They still remain political issues but ones given to unelected judges rather than to parliaments.

These notions were reflected after the August federal election in the suggestions of some of the independent members of the House of Representatives that, if only the two major parties could put aside their differences and cooperate with the independents, many of the problems of government would disappear. In some ways, of course, the Greens represent a variation on this theme. Their policies, which are never costed and which never have to be implemented, are presented as a disinterested alternative to the policies of the two major parties. It is implicit – but never stated – in this position that the Greens' policies represent the common good rather than the policies of those parties, even though 90% of the electorate voted for the two major parties at the last election.

In the US the notion of de-politicising politics has found its ultimate expression in the Tea Party movement. It was common to see in their rallies during the mid-term campaign the signs "Congress: You're Fired". What is to be made of this slogan? There is obviously no problem – either in the US or in Australia – about complaining that the levels taxation set by legislatures are too high or that much of the tax revenue raised is devoted to undeserving causes. But this hardly the same as saying that government has no role to play in the life of the community. Some Tea Party members do not seem to understand that public goods like roads, schools and hospitals fall within the functions of government because even the richest individuals could not arrange for them to be supplied privately. It must be said, however, that governments in both countries have provided some encouragement for these eccentric views by regulatory over kill in some areas – education and communications come to mind in Australia at the federal level – and by the inexorable growth of the bureaucracy.

Churchill remarked that democracy was the worst possible system of government except for all the others. The same might be said about politics as the process of decision-making for governments. It is easy to despair of the conduct of individual politicians or even of whole governments. But it is idle to imagine that anyone would be happier if the decisions were entrusted to some group of platonic guardians supposedly above the world of parties and governments. This will not, however, stop the long-standing quest in both Australia and America for an elysian world without tough choices and free of all divisions within the community.

THE AUSTRALIAN

Thursday, December 11, 2014

VOTERS EXPECT EXPENDITURE, REJECT REVENUE

The rise of special interest representation makes it harder for governments to govern

Robert Menzies won a number of federal elections in the 1950s and early 60s partly on the basis of his question to Labor: "Where is the money coming from?" This was a taunt directed to quite modest proposals by Labor for increased government expenditure on health, education and pensions.

It seems a world away from the present political environment where many sections of the Australian electorate seem to reject any nexus between government revenue and expenditure. Naturally every section of the community is opposed to the idea of increased taxes that would affect themselves but there appears to be a sentiment in many quarters that the resources of government are infinite and not constrained by the amount of funds available on the revenue side of the equation.

This seemingly wide spread view is compounded by the activities of special interest groups in the business, union and welfare sectors who constantly demand increased government spending in their own areas and ferociously resist any suggested reductions of existing government programs that benefit their members. The net result of all this is to exert enormous pressure on budgets at both the federal and State levels.

At the same time, however, voters have significantly weakened the power of most governments in Australia to make budgetary choices about the allocation of increasingly scarce resources. This has occurred through the election to parliamentary upper houses of groups or individual members distinct from the two major parties and largely disinterested in questions of economics. The federal government's difficulties in passing legislation through the Senate, including its budget, over 2014 have been sufficiently documented in the media. Some of the Senators who took their place in July appear to be seriously thought-disordered and provide a standing indictment of the existing system for the election of that body.

But this is not only a problem in the federal sphere. Except for Queensland and the two Territories, the remaining States all have upper houses and all these now, to a greater or lesser degree, have the same problem of groups or individuals other than the two major parties who hold the balance of power. This development has reached new heights – or depths – in Victoria after the election of 29 November with up to a dozen seats in the 40 member Legislative Council to be shared by some or all of the Greens, the DLP, the Shooters and Fishers Party, the Sex Party and the Australian Country Alliance.

None of this means, of course, that the nation is going to collapse tomorrow. As Adam Smith once observed, there is a lot of ruin in any country. And Australia's natural resources, even with some commodity prices falling, will continue to provide a strong base for economic development. But the relentless rise in the health and social security components of the budget means that there is a medium-term problem with the widening gap between committed expenditure and potential revenue. This is the kind of problem that is difficult to address in an unstable political environment. In addition, while everyone complains that governments do not spend enough on major infrastructure projects, this kind of long-term commitment is obviously less likely in such an unpredictable financial climate.

One of the reasons why the electorate finds it difficult to accept the existence of the problem is the long-running period of economic growth that Australia has enjoyed over the last three decades. Over the three previous decades after the war there were fluctuations in the economic cycle that reminded the community that good times were not the natural order. No one wants a return to those days but it is not easy now for governments in Australia to suggest that there is any reason for scaling back their spending.

Although some of the causes differ from country to country, Australia's problems are part of a general trend in Western nations for governments to find it increasingly difficult to actually govern. This is particularly obvious in the US, now that a Democrat administration is confronted by a Republican majority in both houses of the Congress after the November elections. But it is also true to some extent in the United Kingdom, where the Conservatives maintain an uneasy coalition with the Liberal Democrats, and in those members of the European Community with severe economic problems, such as Spain, Italy and Greece. In Australia, however, the combination of governments struggling to control their finances and an electorate growing steadily more cynical and self-interested may eventually lead to much more difficult times in the years ahead.

THE AUSTRALIAN

Wednesday, March 18, 2015

PITY THE POWERLESS POLICYMAKERS

It has become all but impossible to slash government expenditure in the West

Who would want to be a Minister in a federal government in Australia? Because the bad news for both sides of politics is that no real debate is possible on the nation's strategic options within the confines of the existing political system.

To some extent this is because the income-support and welfare measures adopted by Western countries in the post-World War II years have finally collided in all those countries with a declining revenue base. As more people are able to drop out of the working population due to income-support payments and baby-boomers move into government-subsidised retirement, the amount of revenue from income tax will not allow governments to maintain present expenditure levels, even if the marginal rate were to be set at a politically unacceptable level.

An increased GST could, of course, provide a partial remedy on the revenue side but no Australian politician dares to raise this issue. It is said that the GST is a regressive tax and it is true that wealthy individuals probably do not buy many more loaves of bread than less affluent persons. But they do buy much more expensive cars, clothes, wine and so on. As a result, they do pay the lion's share of the GST. And less affluent persons could always be compensated under an increased GST regime by additional income-support payments. But all this is academic if no one on either side of politics is prepared to raise the issue.

The theoretically available option of decreasing any existing income-support payments is simply unrealistic. It has not happened under any government and there seems to be a view held by most of the electorate that these payments can – or should – be increased but can never be decreased. Naturally this view is put forward as well by the welfare sector but this approach is not confined to those groups. Every interest group in the community, from childcare centres to sporting bodies, maintains the view that government expenditure in their area should be substantially increased and that it is simply up to the government to find the money from somewhere.

All this is compounded by the rise in the West of parties who openly defy normal principles of economics, the most dramatic example of this phenomenon being the election in Greece of a government that simply says that debts previously incurred should not be paid if that would interfere with proposed current expenditure. In Australia the Greens are opposed to the so-called capitalist economy while happy to enjoy all of its benefits. They are in favour of increased government expenditure at a whole range of levels while at the same time hostile to most aspects of economic growth that would enable some of those expenditures to be made.

It is a particular problem in Australia that various minor parties with no real interest in financial questions hold the balance of power in the Senate and in most State upper houses. This means that no government can ever assume that legislation raising taxes or cutting existing expenditure programs will actually pass through the parliament. This makes it impossible to frame a budget with a coherent overall strategy aligned to future needs and designed to have some measure of balance between revenue and expenditure.

Even this budgetary impasse, however, is only one aspect of the declining ability of Western governments to legislate for the societies that they have been elected to administer. Those societies are changing but despite and not because of government policies. Ministers now sit atop a swirling sea of interest groups and over-heated electoral concerns without any real capacity to determine the outcome of all these cross currents. To go back to the opening question - who would want to be a Minister in this strange new world? The answer, of course, is any number of people. Perhaps because, as the decision-making powers of politicians have declined over recent decades, their status as minor celebrities – even sometimes major celebrities at the federal level – has increased dramatically. It may be that the shadow has turned out to be more attractive than the substance but none of this will solve the nation's long-term problems.

THE AUSTRALIAN

Tuesday, September 6, 2016

ELECTORAL TIDE IS MOVING AGAINST THE LIBS

Party of Menzies may outlive its usefulness on present trends

Does the Liberal Party have a future in Australia at the national level?

This may seem an extraordinary question to ask in the light of the re-election in July, albeit by the narrowest margin, of the Coalition it leads, and in view of the fact it has been a mainstay of the two-party system in Australia since its formation by Robert Menzies in 1944. It has held office – in Coalition with the National Party, as the Country Party became – for two thirds of that period, although half of that time is accounted for by its 23 unbroken years of government between 1949 and 1972, largely a product of the Labor split in 1955.

It may be, however, that the electoral tide is moving against the Liberals, perhaps slowly but nevertheless inexorably. This is not, it should be noted, because they are a stridently conservative party whose views are largely out of touch with the electorate. The Liberals are at best a centre party – not, however, centre-left like Labor, which in turn is outflanked on the left by the Greens – and the Liberals share with their two rivals widely prevailing views in the Australian community about the substantial role of government in society.

It is largely for this reason that the Liberals have no real solutions to offer to the problem of ever increasing government expenditure combined with relatively static sources of revenue. The problem is caused by interest groups that constantly demand more money for their constituencies and instantly mount a vociferous public complaint if there is any suggestion of a reduction of funds from their existing level. The Liberals – quite naturally – try desperately to pacify these groups by meeting their demands wherever possible. The Nationals are of no assistance in any of this because throughout that party's history its sole objective has been to provide government assistance to its rural constituency, irrespective of the economic merits of these policies.

Despite all this, however, the Liberals cannot match the expenditure proposals of Labor and the Greens. This is a long-term problem when an increasing proportion of the electorate – now almost half – makes no contribution to government by way of taxation but is essentially dependent on government-provided benefits.

Menzies ran several successful election campaigns in the 1950s by asking the question about Labor's spending proposals – very modest by current standards – "Where is the money coming from?" There would be little point in asking this question today because a majority of the electorate has no interest in the answer. It expects governments to find the money somehow and problems of revenue-raising are of no concern. In the long or even medium term, of course, all this will eventually lead to an unsustainable budget deficit. Again, however, this seems to be of no moment to the electorate.

None of this means the Liberals may not win the next federal election or the one after that. All national governments in Australia since Federation have ultimately collapsed politically and been replaced by the electorate. But it may become progressively more difficult for the Liberals to obtain over 50 per cent of the two-party preferred vote in this political climate. It is also clear that they need over 50 per cent of the seats in the House of Representatives in their own right as the Greens and almost any independent will support Labor in the event of a hung parliament. Moreover, the Liberals have to do this without the floods of volunteer workers that opposing groups, such as the ACTU and GetUp, can put into marginal electorates. The Senate is, of course, permanently lost to the Liberals in a way that it is not lost to Labor who can always rely on the Greens when it is in government.

Even when the Liberals do win government, however, they seem happy to largely accept the legislative framework inherited from their opponents. Section 18C of the Racial Discrimination Act has been much discussed but it is a useful symbol. What is the point of being in government if there is not at least an attempt to defend freedom of speech? Over time this passivity on the part of the Liberals allows their opponents to determine the political agenda and so make it harder each time for a Liberal government to depart from the existing culture.

This political climate is not confined to Australia but can be observed in Western Europe and even in the US. It is true that nominally conservative parties have held office in, for example, the United Kingdom and Spain, but they have pursued very much centrist policies. The demands on government are increasing so rapidly in all these countries that it has become very difficult to resist them. It may be, therefore, that centre left or even further left parties are better placed to win office in most Western countries in the immediate future. In any event, it seems that the federal Liberal party in this country is entering a very difficult period of its history.

THE AUSTRALIAN,

Wednesday, December 7, 2016

THE FULL HOUSE THEY DIDN'T SEE

Founding fathers to blame for a Senate that will probably never function properly

How about setting tax rates by a random selection of numbers in the way Powerball lotteries are drawn?

This could hardly produce more bizarre results than the negotiations in the Senate in the last sitting week of the parliament when income tax rates of 10.5, 13, 15 and 19.5 per cent for foreign agricultural workers were all put forward and rejected before 15 per cent was adopted. This followed a series of amendments that partially emasculated the legislation establishing the Australian Building and Construction Commission which, even then, was only passed after the government agreed to concessions on the entirely unrelated question of water rights in the Murray-Darling Basin.

The current Senate demonstrates what has become increasingly clear in the post-war years – that the form of the upper house established by the Constitution in 1901 was the single greatest failure of foresight on the part of those who drafted the basis for Federation. The founding fathers took as their model the US Senate but failed to appreciate that two senators from each of what was then 48 American States was a very different proposition than six senators – now 12 – from each of six Australian States. The current US Senate essentially reflects the two-party system in that country with no minor parties and only two independents. In contrast, at the federal election in July 20 cross-bench senators were elected – more than a quarter of the total of 76 upper house members.

This is the culmination of the emergence of minor parties and independents in the Senate over the last 60 years. The first of these groups was the Democratic Labor Party, following the Labor split in 1955, to be followed between 1977 and 2008 by the Australian Democrats and then by the Greens. In all that time there were only three very brief periods in the life of the Menzies, Fraser and Howard administrations where the government of the day had a majority in the Senate and could rely on its legislation being passed intact.

This problem has been considerably accentuated by the failure of a now almost forgotten referendum in 1967. Section 24 of the Constitution requires that the number of members in the House of Representatives be, as nearly as possible, no more than twice the number of members in the Senate. In May 1967 the Holt government asked the electorate in a referendum to break this nexus so that the House of Representatives could be increased while leaving the number of senators as they were. The referendum was comfortably lost in all States but New South Wales, despite being supported by the two major parties, after a campaign by dissident Liberal senators who argued that this would decrease the power of the upper house. It would certainly have decreased the power of minor parties and independents in the long run because the larger the number of senators to be elected from each State the smaller the quota of votes that is necessary to be elected. As it happens, the size of the House of Representatives – and so the Senate also – was not increased to their present numbers until 1985.

It is obvious that there is not the slightest chance in the foreseeable future of a government obtaining a majority in the Senate when it comes to office. This means that every significant piece of legislation that it wishes to enact must be the subject of endless negotiation with minor parties or single independents, many of whom have obsessive agendas far removed from the major issues confronting any government. In particular, these groups and individuals have shown little interest in the ever-widening gap in Australia between government expenditure and government revenue. They normally vote against any cuts in government funding because any reductions of expenditure in any sector of the community is unpopular with those affected. So who wants to be unpopular?

Is there any prospect of constitutional change to deal with the monster that the Senate has become? Probably not. The two major parties did combine before the last election to change the way in which preferences were directed in Senate elections but, while this may have affected the composition of the cross-bench, it did not result in a decrease in its size – it actually increased. Given the number of senators now elected from each State there is very little that the two major parties could do to deal with the current situation, even in the unlikely event of their agreement on a solution.

THE SPECTATOR AUSTRALIA

30 September 2017

INSANE EXPECTATIONS

What the public do and don't demand of our politicians has changed - and not for the best

Politics has always been a notoriously unstable activity but over recent years this has been accentuated by several long-accepted rules being stood on their head.

The first of these rules was the notion that governments would be rewarded by the electorate for sound economic management or even for presiding over good economic conditions, whatever their contribution to those conditions might have been. But voters in Western nations, and particularly in Australia, no longer seem to display this gratitude. Unaware of the booms and busts of economic history, they assume that endless periods of sustained growth combined with low inflation and low interest rates are the norm. They give governments little credit for either creating or for not counteracting these circumstances. So in the 2007 election the Howard government was wiped out despite a range of positive economic conditions, including a budget surplus. It is true that after 11 years there was a strong element of time for a change in the result but the electorate seemed quite indifferent to the issue of economic management.

At the New Zealand election in late September the National Party government lost its majority in the parliament despite there being 4% growth in the economy in the last financial year, less than 5% unemployment and a budget surplus. The New Zealand system of multi-member electorates makes it difficult for any party to obtain an absolute majority in the parliament but it is something of a puzzle as to why almost 46% of those voting opted for a change of government, given the extraordinarily favourable state of the economy.

The second rule of politics that appears to have been completely overturned in recent times is that the electorate would be rightly suspicious of fiscal irresponsibility. In the 1950s and into the 1960s Prime Minister Menzies continually attacked Labor's spending proposals – very modest by current standards – by asking "Where is the money coming from?". And this seemed to strike a chord with the electorate. But there would be no point in any politician asking such a question today when the attitude of much of the community is that there should be increased government spending in every area of administration and that it is simply up to the government of the day to find the money. Many voters seem to make no connection between notions of revenue and expenditure. They violently resist any proposals for increased taxation, at least insofar as it applies to themselves, but demand increased expenditure, at least in relation to anything that affects their own interests.

This attitude seems to be based in part on the fantasy that somewhere in the community there is a group of extremely rich individuals who could fund all government programs if properly taxed. It is no doubt true that the very wealthy arrange their affairs so as not to pay significant tax but, even if all their assets were confiscated tomorrow, this would not make a meaningful contribution to the revenue side of the budget. There is a similar fantasy about multinational companies and their tax contributions. This is an area where governments in all countries need to do more work but any increased revenue from these sources could never bridge the gap in Australia between taxation and expenditure.

As a result of all this, the idea of a balanced budget has no electoral appeal. In Britain's election earlier this year, Labour leader Jeremy Corbyn simply promised massive new spending programs and ignored any questions as to how they would be funded. Labour did not win the election but it substantially increased its vote on the previous poll. This is a long-term problem for the Liberals in the Australian context because they can never out-promise or out-spend Labor and the Greens and they feel obliged to make some efforts, although not very successful, to reduce the budget deficit.

The third political rule that seems to have gone by the board is that there was a division under the Australian Constitution between federal and State functions. One area that had always been the responsibility of the States – and for which the Commonwealth has no power under the Constitution – was the supply of power. Now there is said to be a crisis in relation to the provision of electricity and everyone assumes that it is up to the federal government to find a solution. Education, always a State responsibility and one for which the Commonwealth has no constitutional power, is another area where federal funding and regulation is seen as the solution for all problems in schools and universities. In keeping with the notion that the federal government must be concerned with every aspect of Australian society, a Senate inquiry was established in early September into the decision by the Australian Rugby Union to remove its Western Australian team from the Super Fifteen competition. What on earth as such a decision by a sporting body got to do with the national government? Needless to say there is no mention of sport in the Constitution.

The fourth rule to be discarded is the idea that experience in public administration is normally a requirement, or at least highly desirable, for national leadership. This change is largely a product of the cult of celebrity and has resulted in a range of world leaders with little or no experience in government, including President Trump, Canada's Justin Trudeau and France's Emmanuel Macron. In some ways Bob Hawke was an early Australian example of this phenomenon, although Hawke turned out to be a very able administrator. More generally, however, this development reflects the electorate's impatience with the traditional constraints of politics and government. It reflects a feeling – almost invariably wrong – that a celebrity figure can sweep aside all these limitations and introduce dramatic solutions to long-standing problems. It is yet another example of the increasing gap between reality and the expectations of the electorate. Most politicians, of course, are too frightened to tell people something that they don't want to hear so there is no real prospect of a return to reality in the immediate future.

THE AUSTRALIAN

Thursday, April 12, 2018

CULTURAL TAKEOVER TRAPPING LIBS ON THE OUTER

In the face of growing political correctness, Coalition Newspoll numbers are not so bad

The most surprising thing about the last 30 Newspolls is that in today's political climate the Coalition still holds 47 to 48 per cent of the two-party preferred vote. This may seem an unusual proposition, but the Liberals face some significant present and long-term disadvantages in the Australian political system, particularly at the national level.

One of these disadvantages is that the Liberals are largely considered unfashionable and almost disreputable amongst the politically correct class that dominates most public and private institutions. For most of the country's political history the non-Labor parties were considered the respectable side of politics and until the 1980s they usually won federal elections. But over the last 30 years the politically correct class has taken control of most of the media, universities and schools, almost all cultural institutions, the boards of many public companies and even major sporting bodies. The members of this class generally would not stoop to involvement in party politics but their views on such questions as border security, power generation and freedom of speech mean that they are broadly unsympathetic to the Liberals. Because this group controls so much of the public debate in Australia, it is the Coalition that has become the less fashionable and less respectable alternative.

Which is not to say that it cannot win any future federal elections, including the next one, given the system of preferential voting means that ultimately almost all votes for seats in the House of

Representatives come back to one of the two main parties, so neither of them can be far out of any particular election. But the notion of the Liberals being unfashionable appears to have had a particular impact on young people. There seems to be a view in this group that joining the Young Liberals is somewhat akin to becoming involved with a fringe religious cult, whereas signing up with the Young Labor or the Greens is socially quite acceptable.

Another major change that has occurred over recent decades is that on economic issues a Liberal party has become a centrist party facing a centre-left electorate. It is hard to recall that in the 1950s and 1960s Robert Menzies made political hay during election campaigns with Labor's rather modest spending proposals, solemnly asking "Where is the money coming from?" As it happens, the modern Liberals have embraced increasing government expenditure but they can never really outbid Labor and the Greens in this area. Meanwhile the electorate sees no problem with even greater government expenditure in every sector of the community as long as this involves the payment of no additional tax on their part. The obvious gap between revenue and expenditure is seen to be the government's problem and it is up to the authorities to produce a budgetary magic pudding. When Liberals do on occasion speak about the need for a balanced budget and some spending restraints they simply seem mean-minded to a community that has enjoyed decades of unbroken economic growth.

These are cultural problems for the Liberals but there are some further difficulties posed by the electoral system. In the case of votes for the House of Representatives, the Coalition not only needs to get more than 50 per cent of the two-party preferred vote but also an absolute majority of seats, given the fact that the minor parties and independents almost invariably opt for a Labor side in a hung parliament, as they did in 2010. In relation to the Senate, the voting system ensures the election of enough minor parties and independents to prevent either of the main parties gaining a majority in its own right. Labor, however, can usually depend on the Greens to pass its legislation, whereas the Coalition struggles to implement its policies despite endless negotiations with the non-Green cross-benchers.

In terms of personnel on the ground during election campaigns, the Liberals cannot compete with the numbers Labor can assemble from the union movement and supporting groups like GetUp! In addition, the financial contributions to Labor from its union affiliates is substantial and steady. It might be thought that these could be matched by contributions to the Liberals from the business community but, as already noted, many large corporations are no longer sympathetic to the Liberals and, in any event, are keen to hedge their bets by contributing to both sides of politics. For the same reason, they are unwilling to speak out publicly in support of Liberal policies, even when those policies would be beneficial to the business sector.

All this suggests a bleak future for the Liberals at the national level, but it must be remembered that Australian elections are two-horse races and no one should ever bet too heavily on that kind of contest.

PRIME MINISTERS AND THEIR RIVALS

These pieces, mostly in the form of book reviews, assess the lives of a number of Australia's post-war Prime Ministers – Menzies, McMahon, Whitlam, Keating and Turnbull. There are also examinations of Menzies' chief rival in the 1950s – Opposition leader H V Evatt – and a person who, although never elected to any public office, had an enormous impact on Australian politics in the 1950s and 1960s – B A Santamaria

PRIME MINISTERS AND THEIR RIVALS

SYDNEY MORNING HERALD

10 September 1988

I'LL HANDLE THIS IN MY OWN WAY

The Spycatcher Trial by Malcolm Turnbull

Like Rex Mottram in *Brideshead Revisited*, Malcolm Turnbull is always at the centre of the action. In the course of a single week he jousts with High Court judges, confers with Cabinet ministers and negotiates billion dollar deals for tycoon clients.

This book is not just the story of the *Spycatcher* case but also the autobiography – so far – of Young Malcolm. It is Turnbull's answer to Churchill's *My Early Life*.

The story of the trial, however, began in 1986 when the British Government took proceedings in the New South Wales Supreme Court to prevent the publication of the memoirs of former MI5 officer, Peter Wright. The legal basis of this claim was that Wright was in breach of a contract he had made not to reveal anything about his period with MI5 and/or that he had a legal duty to keep this information confidential because of the circumstances in which he had acquired it. The discussion of the issues before the court is central to the book and in this respect Turnbull is certainly an unusual lawyer. He writes clearly and intelligibly about legal questions, in a way non-lawyers can readily understand.

In taking this action the British Government was acting in a long tradition of support for the Whitehall mandarin view that nothing concerning the workings of Government should be public knowledge.

The concern to keep the affairs of these organisations private is perhaps understandable in view of the propensity of security services in all countries, including Britain, for attracting unstable personalities who have difficulty distinguishing fact from fantasy.

Wright's own book is another round in the great mole hunt. Its essential thesis is that Sir Roger Hollis, who was Director-General of MI5 from 1956 to 1965, was a Soviet agent. This may or may not be true but no-one, including Wright, has ever produced any hard evidence in support of the allegation. It is something of an irony that the processes of law were invoked to enable Wright's book to be published. Wright and his MI5 colleagues did not hesitate to engage in illegal conduct in the course of many of their operations over the years.

Turnbull's inclination early in the case was to settle it by going straight to the top. He telephoned his old friend, Jonathan Aitken, who is a Tory member of the House of Commons, explaining:

> Jonathan knows everyone in London ... I knew that if anyone could get the ear of the Prime Minister he could.

Turbull did not beat around the bush:

> I have a great admiration for Thatcher, Jonathan, as you well know, but she must be told that the case is now on a collision course.

The British Government was unmoved and the case proceeded to trial before Mr Justice Powell in the NSW Supreme Court. The centrepiece of the book is a series of highlights from Turnbull's cross-examination of Sir Robert Armstrong, the British Cabinet Secretary. Armstrong emerged from this cross-examination without a shred of credibility.

One of the most depressing aspects of the case was the intervention of the Australian Government in support of the British claim, by means of evidence given by Michael Codd, head of the Prime Minister's Department in Canberra. It was hardly a surprise to learn that Sir Humphrey Appleby has his antipodean counterparts who espouse the view that information is a dangerous commodity. Mr Justice Powell was not impressed, describing some of Codd's evidence as "complete and utter moonshine".

The trial resulted in a victory for Wright. Mr Justice Powell held that there had been no breach of contract by Wright and that the British Government had been unable to show that any damage would result from any confidential information disclosed. The British Government appealed to the NSW Court of Appeal, which also found for Wright, deciding that a foreign government had no legal basis for a claim of this kind in an Australian Court. The British Government then trekked on to the High Court, which came to the same conclusion.

When *Spycatcher* finally hit bookstores, the British Government stupidly had already ensured that it would be a runaway best seller. So compensation no doubt for the managing director of the British publisher who queried Turnbull's judgment at one point in the case. The response was obvious:

> Keep your head down and leave it to me. I'll handle this in my own way … shut up.

Move over Rex Mottram.

THE AUSTRALIAN

14-15 April 2007

CHURCH AND STATE: SANTAMARIA, MANNIX AND THE WESTMINSTER SYSTEM

In the early 1950s I went with my father to a function after Sunday Mass at the local parish church in Mont Albert in Melbourne's eastern suburbs. The speaker at the function was B A Santamaria and he spoke about Vietnam. Not many people were talking about Vietnam in Australia at that time but he stressed the importance of the survival of the regime in South Vietnam and the qualities of its Catholic leader, Ngo Dinh Diem. I was struck by the speaker's intensity but, unlike most the audience, I retained some scepticism. This was because I was in the unusual position of growing up in a Catholic family but one that did not support the DLP. Many Catholics, of course, not only supported the DLP in an electoral sense but also were actively involved in its affairs and in those of the Church organisation effectively led by Santamaria – the Movement.

In recent weeks Santamaria's role in post-war Australian politics has been defended by federal Health Minister, Tony Abbott, and attacked by former Victorian Premier, John Cain. The origins of Labor's 1955 Split were complex but there is no doubt that two individuals played a large part in the events that led up to the division in the ALP and the formation of the DLP – Santamaria and his mentor, Daniel Mannix, Catholic Archbishop of Melbourne. What is remarkable, however, is that, despite their impact on Australian political life, neither Santamaria nor Mannix ever accepted the notion of parliamentary democracy under the Westminster system.

It is true that, as a matter of theory, England had an established church but, even in that country, and certainly in Australia, the theory of parliamentary democracy precluded the direction of members of parliament and of government policy by private institutions. It is clear, however, that both Santamaria and Mannix looked forward in the late 1940s and early 1950s to Labor governments – at both the State and federal level – where a majority of members were amenable to the implementation of policies that accorded with the social and economic tenets of the Church.

In an extraordinary letter, written to Mannix in 1952, Santamaria suggested that eventually the Movement would be able to "completely transform the leadership of the Labor Movement and introduce into the federal and state spheres large numbers of members who possess a clear realisation of what Australia demands of them and the will to carry it out". It was implicit in this approach that any Catholic members of parliament who personally agreed with the teachings of the Church but did not think that these should be imposed on the non-Catholic majority in the community should be removed from their parliamentary office and also deprived of any role in the affairs of the Church.

This had been the situation for many years in Mannix's own Ireland and also in Spain and Portugal. It had also been true, to a lesser degree, in Italy. In contrast to England and the United States, these countries did not proceed on the assumption of a secular and pluralist society where questions of faith and morals were left to individuals. On the contrary, the dogmas of the Church - in such areas as divorce, abortion and contraception – were imposed on the whole community by the government, including those members of the community who were not adherents of the Church. Santamaria was a strong supporter of some aspects of American foreign policy but not of Thomas Jefferson's strong belief in the separation of church and state which had been embodied in the United States Constitution.

Mannix's view on this question was illustrated by his reaction to a statement issued in 1943 by Cardinal Gilroy and his Anglican counterpart which, in a rather general fashion, condemned authoritarian regimes, whether fascist or communist. It said that "freedom of worship and freedom to propagate religious beliefs" were fundamental rights. Mannix protested about the insertion of this phrase, saying to Gilroy that there was only one true Church and therefore no right to propagate contrary religious dogmas.

This view of the Australian political system also led to the ready acceptance of exerting influence within one of the two major political parties by means of an essentially secret organisation. As a result, when Santamaria and the Movement finally became part of the public debate, they had an aura of mystery and intrigue that inevitably made it more difficult for them to defend their position to those outside their closed group.

It was essentially for these same reasons that Santamaria and Mannix took a view of the Second World War that seems remarkable in retrospect. On the fact of it, this conflict would be one of a few in modern history where the issues were so clear. But in October 1940 Mannix said that he "believed that Hitler's victories were ephemeral and [that] Russia was a greater danger than Germany. The word "ephemeral" is extraordinary when it is recalled that at this time Hitler controlled Europe from Warsaw to Calais and, two months earlier, the Battle of Britain had narrowly staved off a cross-channel invasion by the Germans. But for Mannix the Soviet Union, which posed no threat to Western Europe, was still the real enemy – because it was the enemy of the Church. As we now know, of course, Hitler's view of the Church was no different from that of Stalin. Hitler had, however, cultivated some of its leaders in Germany and preferred to deal finally with it at a later time.

As Paul Ormonde has pointed out, there is scarcely a reference in Santamaria's own memoirs to the Second World War. Ormonde quotes Santamaria as saying much later that: "Nazism could only win if it won military victory. Communism could win through international organisation founded on ideology." One problem about this statement is that Nazism is a rather meaningless term. The real problem was the nation of Germany and in 1940 it almost won the war by military victories. Another problem is that if, by Communism, Santamaria largely meant the Soviet Union, it is quite clear that for a variety off reasons, including Stalin's purges, it posed no threat to other nations in 1940.

Santamaria's attitude to so many of these issues was perhaps summed up in his statement in 1952 that one of the great evils of modern history was the birth of the "modern liberal democratic secular state" in Europe in the years between 1750 and 1848. Think of the notions that are rejected in this statement:

- modern
- liberal
- democratic
- secular

Of these four, perhaps the most striking rejection is that of the idea of democracy. But it was perfectly natural that Santamaria would reject this concept which, rightly or wrongly, has no place in the government of the Church. If, of course, one accepts Mannix's view that there is only truth and error, then the view of a majority, however large, are irrelevant, unless they also represent the truth.

These views may seem startling in 2007 but Santamaria was not the only person to hold them in the 1940s and the 1950s. Evelyn Waugh, for example, would have shared these opinions, despite coming from a very different background from Santamaria and Mannix. There are, of course, persons in many countries, including Australia, who still hold these views today.

But the importance of Mannix and Santamaria holding these views was that they were in positions of real political power in the late 1940s and the early 1950s leading up to the Split. It is true that they held no elective office but they had control of the resources of the Church in Victoria. This meant that very large reserves of money and personnel were available to support the work of the Industrial Groups in the Labor Party. Although the Anglican Church may have had a larger membership, many of these were members in name only. Otherwise, the Catholic Church was the largest single organisation in the community by a considerable margin. Moreover, it was high organised through the parish structure and intensely hierarchical. It was hardly an accident that the Split started in Victoria and was much more serious in that State than in any other.

There can be – and has been – dispute as to the importance of Mannix and Santamaria in the events that brought about the Split. It is no doubt true that, if Labor had won the 1954 election – and it was not far off winning it – the Split may very well have been averted. It is also true to say that Evatt was probably the worst possible person to be Labor leader at the time and contributed in large measure to the break-down in relations between the various groups within the party. But there can be little doubt that the role of Mannix and Santamaria was pivotal in the Split and that this period of Australian history cannot be fully appreciated without a close examination of these two very unusual men and their rejection of the Westminster system of parliamentary democracy.

THE SYDNEY MORNING HERALD

March 13-14, 2010

ROSE-COLOURED VIEW OF A CHEQUERED LIFE

The memoirs of a controversial former prime minister lack light and shade and are, in places, hard to believe

Malcolm Fraser: The Political Memoirs by Malcolm Fraser and Margaret Simons

Margaret Simons is a modern-day version of Pollyanna. She has written what is essentially a third-person biography of Malcolm Fraser, although it is styled as his memoirs. And she has looked at his political life through the softest of rose-coloured spectacles.

Fraser's early years reveal no dramas in growing up among Victoria's Western District grazing families and Melbourne's clubland. Then to Oxford and the Federal Parliament in 1955 at the age of 26 as member for the family's local seat.

Fraser spent the next decade on the backbenches of the Menzies government until he was made minister for the army by Harold Holt in 1966 and then minister for defence by John Gorton in 1969. He was, therefore, at the absolute forefront of Australia's involvement in the Vietnam War. He now says that the war was a "mistake" but that these were "innocent days". Even as a backbencher he had high-level meetings in Washington in 1964 but suggests that they left him quite "mystified and concerned about the way in which policy was being made". Most unbelievably of all, he says that he learnt for the first time in 1995, when reading Robert McNamara's memoirs, that the US administration had been involved in the coup that led to the deposing and assassination of the South Vietnamese Prime Minister,

Ngo Dinh Diem in 1963. Can this be for real?

After bringing about the removal of John Gorton as prime minister in 1971 and Billy Snedden as opposition leader in 1975, Fraser finally became Liberal leader. Then in November 1975, he was responsible for the most cynical and unscrupulous exercise in Australian political history – the blocking of the budget by the Senate and the forcing of an early election. This is not, of course, to defend the Whitlam government's situation at that time. Quite apart from anything else, the loans affair provided strong evidence that the prime minister and several senior ministers had taken leave of their senses. The government would have been annihilated at the election due in a year. But that hardly justified the deliberate subversion of the electoral process. Of course, the governor general, Sir John Kerr, behaved foolishly in not confronting Whitlam with the alternatives. Kerr said later that he feared he would be dismissed but then he would have been the victim, not Whitlam. As it happened, he became the fall guy for the events of November 1975 and was driven drunkenly from public life. But all this occurred at Fraser's instigation. It was his decision and his responsibility. At least in this case, unlike Vietnam, Fraser says that he would do it all over again.

Then comes the largest part of this enormous book – Fraser's period as prime minister from December 1975 to March 1983. This is essentially a rebuttal of the often-voiced criticism that Fraser presided over what was largely a do-nothing administration, even though he had a majority in the Senate as well as the lower house for most of this period.

This is a difficult case to argue. As the book demonstrates, there was some minor deregulation of the financial system by the Fraser government but all of the major reforms took place during the Hawke-Keating period – the floating of the dollar, the entry of foreign banks and the removal of restrictions on bank interest rates. In the same way, there were no significant reductions in tariffs during the Fraser years and this also had to wait for the next Labor government. Nor was there any serious attempt at tax reform over this period. It is true that this was also a failing by the Hawke-Keating administration, although no fault of Keating who wanted to introduce a GST and could not get the support of his colleagues. A GST was, of course, introduced by the Howard government but it also avoided the more difficult question of reform to the income tax regime.

The book portrays Fraser as a tireless defender of human rights on the international stage. This concern did not, however, extend to the large number of Timorese who were killed by the Indonesians in the second half of the 1970s. When the Indonesian invasion took place in December 1975 Fraser, in his first days as Prime Minister, sent a note of effective acquiescence to President Suharto. When the matter came before the United Nations, Australia abstained when resolutions condemning the Indonesian invasion were passed. Fraser now says that Australia was "manipulated" by the Indonesians. If so, they were certainly very successful as manipulators.

One of Fraser's most active international roles was in the negotiations over the future of Zimbabwe in the late 1970s. Fraser pushed for a solution that resulted in Robert Mugabe becoming the leader of an independent Zimbabwe in 1980. Mugabe said that he was "enchanted" by Fraser. It would be unfair to blame Fraser and the others involved in the negotiations for what has happened in Zimbabwe but the fact is that Mugabe turned out to be not just a monster but a totally incompetent one at that. Out of office in the late 1980s Fraser was also heavily involved in the negotiations between the Commonwealth and the South African government leading up to black rule.

Over recent years Fraser has become something of a darling of the chattering classes because of his attacks on American foreign policy, Israel's role in the Middle East and domestic legislation dealing with terrorism. The book sets out these views as yet another example of Fraser's nobility. But this is really the problem with the whole work. Biography – or autobiography – whichever this book is, needs a mixture of light and shade. There is too much rose-coloured light in this account of what was in fact a very chequered career.

THE AUSTRALIAN

Thursday, November 6, 2014

WHITLAM'S LONG SHADOW

He was the Labor movement's hero and martyr, and achieved a unique status

Those persons outside the Sydney Town Hall yesterday who booed Tony Abbott and John Howard when they arrived at the Whitlam memorial service not only showed bad taste but a poor sense of history, particularly as they no doubt welcomed Malcolm Fraser.

In many ways Whitlam's most successful period of public life was as opposition leader between 1967 and 1972. When he took over that role, Labor had been out of office for 18 years. Whitlam's great achievement was to restore credibility in the eyes of the electorate, including many Liberal voters who had never considered voting otherwise. This was no easy task. It might be thought from much of the commentary that the 1972 election was a landslide. In fact, the result was close despite the Coalition government having been in office for 23 years and being led by the unimpressive William McMahon.

The next three years were stormy ones in Canberra. True, the government was subjected to bloody-minded obstruction by the Senate, where it never had the numbers, and this gradually eroded its confidence in its ability to govern. It also met fierce opposition from the states and private interest groups in a way that now seems bizarre. The Australian Medical Association, for example, fought the introduction of Medibank tooth and nail, even though this system of universal health insurance was never designed to affect the existing position of doctors.

Yet the internal affairs of the government were often chaotic. In part this was a product of the 23 years of opposition, which meant that no ministers had any experience of government. The Cabinet also included extremely willful personalities, including Jim Cairns, Lionel Murphy and Rex Connor, who would have tested the management skills of any prime minister. The nadir was the Loans Affair, an attempt to borrow in secret $4 billion through fly-by-night operators. This absurd exercise significantly affected John Kerr's view of the government as he was concerned that he had been involved in some illegality by signing, as governor general, the documents authorising a loan. It also provided the public justification for Fraser's decision to block supply in October 1975 in an attempt to force the government to an election.

It is important to remember that the author of the events of November 1975 was Malcolm Fraser and not Sir John Kerr. Despite its many problems, the Whitlam government was entitled to go through until the next election where it almost certainly would have been wiped out at the polls. Fraser and his colleagues engaged in an utterly cynical and irresponsible use of their numbers in the Senate to bring about a political crisis. This was simple greed for ministerial positions that would have almost certainly been available in a year's time after an election.

Kerr's conduct was too clever by half. He was certainly clever in his deception of Whitlam and his meticulous planning for the removal of the government. But he lost the historical battle by his failure to warn Whitlam of what he was considering. This would not have been a pleasant conversation but it would have given Kerr the high ground and completely altered his role in these events. Any attempt to remove the governor-general, would have only worsened the government's position in the eyes of the electorate. Kerr quickly became a sad figure, driven from official life, drunk in public and abandoned by those he had brought to office.

Fraser, of course, became prime minister but his eight years in government are generally considered, even by his own party, to have been largely wasted. He failed to make the significant changes, particularly in national economic policy, initiated during the Hawke and Keating governments. Whitlam, however, became a martyr and hero in the Labor movement, achieving a status that even Hawke and Keating could never quite attain. Whitlam certainly cast a long shadow in modern Australian history.

SYDNEY MORNING HERALD

October 8-9, 2016

LUCIFER-LIKE AMBITION COSTS A MAN AND A NATION

EVATT: A Life by John Murphy

Herbert Vere Evatt is one of the big figures of Australian political – and legal – history. But he has proved an elusive subject for four previous biographers. Now comes a new life by Melbourne University politics professor John Murphy.

Evatt was born in 1894 into a middle class family that managed hotels, and his life until the early 1950s was an unending series of glittering prizes. Driven to succeed, particularly by his demanding mother, he took every academic award at Fort Street High School and at Sydney University, graduating in philosophy and law, and was also president of the students' association. In 1919 he went to the Bar but paused briefly in 1920 from this relentless progress to marry Mary Alice Sheffer with whom he would adopt two children.

In 1925 he was elected as a Labor member for Balmain in the NSW Legislative Assembly. Like many of his colleagues, however, he fell out with Premier Jack Lang. He was re-elected as an independent in 1927 but essentially returned to the law, taking silk as a KC in 1929. In 1930, he was appointed by the federal Labor government to the High Court, still the youngest ever judge of the court at 36. The poisonous relationships on the court are illustrated by a letter – quoted in the book – to his fellow judge by Chief Justice Latham: "Dear Evatt, I acknowledge receipt of your letter of Thursday last – much of it is meaningless to me. Yours sincerely, John Latham".

Independently wealthy because of his wife's money, Evatt could afford to take gambles. In 1940 he stood down from the High Court and was elected to the House of Representatives. As soon as he arrived in Canberra Evatt began to undermine Labor's leader, John Curtin, and to make private overtures to Prime Minister Robert Menzies. The Menzies government fell in 1941, however, and Curtin took over as Prime Minister with Evatt as Attorney General and Minister for External Affairs, posts he held until the end of 1949. This was the career of a man who was, to quote Sam Houston's description of Confederate president Jefferson Davis, "as ambitious as Lucifer".

The book deals fully with Evatt's ministerial period which contained some mixed results. As Attorney General he failed to achieve a significant increase in federal powers when all but one of five referendums were lost. And he lost the cases in the High Court and the Privy Council, when the government's bank nationalisation legislation was struck down by these courts. He had addressed the Privy Council for 22 days and two of the judges died before the decision came down – bored to death by some accounts.

But on the international stage Evatt cut a large figure, particularly at the drafting of the United Nations' constitution in 1945 and with his election as president of the UN General Assembly in 1948. Despite spending much of these years out of Australia, he was chosen as Labor's deputy leader – to Prime Minister Chifley – after the 1946 election. In the 1949 election Menzies led the Liberals to government and won again in 1951. Six weeks after the election Chifley died and Evatt became Labor leader unopposed. As the book makes clear, the combination of Evatt's insatiable ambition and his paranoia about threats to his position meant that this would always be an unstable period for Labor. But in 1955 came the Split that was to produce the Democratic Labor Party and keep Labor out of office until 1972. There were many issues and personalities that led to this explosion, including, of course, B A Santamaria's attempt to capture the ALP for one section of the Catholic church, but it was Evatt who lit the fuse in October 1954 by publically attacking the Santamaria forces that he had previously courted. Murphy downplays Evatt's role in the Split in comparison with some earlier historians, like Robert Murray, but concedes that his lack of political skills was an important factor.

Evatt seemed unhinged by Labor's very narrow loss in the 1954 election which he attributed to Menzies' use of the defection of Soviet agent Vladimir Petrov. In the Royal Commission into espionage in Australia that followed the election three of Evatt's staff were named and two of these were represented before the Commission by Evatt himself until his right to appear was withdrawn by the Commission. The account of Evatt's obsession with conspiracies against himself is one of the most striking parts of the book.

It was all downhill from here. The 1955 and 1958 elections were lost. To get Evatt out of the federal leadership the NSW Labor government was forced to appoint him NSW Chief Justice in 1960. Already suffering from advanced dementia, this role was quite beyond him. He retired from the Bench in 1962 and died in 1965. This comprehensive work is likely to remain the standard biography of Evatt for some time, although there may still be room for further exploration of an extraordinary character who was ultimately so destructive to himself, his party and the nation.

THE SYDNEY INSTITUTE

April 12, 2017

AN EXPLODING LIGHT ON LABOR'S HILL

Paul Keating: The Big-picture Leader by Troy Bramston

In 1986 I was one of the 99 delegates to the ALP National Conference in Hobart as a member of the NSW group. On the last night of the conference a number of the NSW delegates met for a drink in one of the rooms of the Wrest Point Casino where the conference had been held. At one point Paul Keating made a speech that was filmed by an ABC *Four Corners* unit. It was making a program about the conference that was broadcast the following week.

I took no notice at the time, but when the program went to air, I could be seen for a few seconds standing in a corner of the room. Quite a number of people in the Labor Party whom I had known for many years simply stopped speaking to me. They saw Keating as a devil figure who was intent on destroying all the party's traditions. Only a few years later, when he was Prime Minister, the same people adopted Keating as a hero and still accord him that status. This was something of a lesson in the vagaries of human behaviour but it is also an illustration of the strong passions that Keating stirred both inside and outside the Labor Party over his political career.

This political career began when Keating won pre-selection for the safe Labor seat of Blaxland in late 1968 at the age of 24. Bramston's account of the pre-selection is exhaustive and reminiscent of Robert Caro's extraordinary detailed account of Lyndon Johnson's victory in the 1948 Senate race in Texas. As in the case of Johnson's success, there have been allegations then and since that Keating did not have a majority of the votes but, in this case, he was awarded the victory by the Labor administration in New South Wales. The truth is that most

Labor pre-selections then and now are contests in who can break the most rules and get away with it and it can be assumed that Blaxland was no different.

In any event, Keating arrived in Canberra in October 1969 after an election where Labor made up enormous ground from its crushing defeat of 1966 but still remained in opposition as it had been for 20 years. Dick Klugman, who was elected at the same time as the member for Prospect, used to tell the story of how the new NSW members were addressed by Whitlam who remarked what a good thing it was that some professional men – Klugman was a doctor – were coming into the Parliament instead of the usual ignorant Irish Catholics from NSW Labor. As an Irish Catholic, Keating was no doubt bemused.

Keating was the youngest member of the parliament and he was a young man in a hurry. When the Whitlam government came to office in December 1972, he stood for election to the ministry and just missed out on the last vacancy. When the government was re-elected in May 1974 he stood again for the ministry but did not come so close. Keating was finally elected to the ministry in October 1975, as Minister for Northern Australia – 21 days before the government was dismissed.

The great saga of Labor's next seven and a half years in opposition was, of course, the struggle between Hayden and Hawke for the leadership and the book gives a graphic account of this conflict. Hayden was largely deprived of his opportunity to become Prime Minister by a vote of the Caucus in June 1977 when Whitlam defeated Hayden in a leadership ballot by two votes. Keating voted for Hayden but Whitlam's utterly irresponsible and selfish behaviour in clinging on to the leadership meant that the election result in 1977 was the same as for 1975. Although Hayden went close to winning in 1980 and would have done so in 1983, he was forced out of the leadership by Hawke on the day that the 1983 election was called.

Keating had spent almost all the opposition period as shadow minister for resources and energy but shortly before the 1983 election he became shadow Treasurer and then the Treasurer in the new government. As the book makes clear, the relationship between Hawke and Keating, although often convivial in the early years, was bound to end in tears. Keating thought he had got to where he was by more than 20 years of bloody conflicts whereas, in his mind, Hawke had been handed on a silver platter the post of ACTU presidency, a seat in Parliament and then the Labor leadership. Hawke, on the other hand, considered that he had always been destined to be Labor leader and would always remain the party's best prospect for winning any given election. As the government continued in office and Keating saw himself as its major player, he became increasingly impatient to assume its leadership and pressed Hawke to name his departure date.

One of the earliest clashes between these two prima donnas occurred at the national taxation summit in July 1985 when Hawke failed to support Keating's proposal for a broad-based consumption tax. Keating regarded this as a public humiliation and never forgave Hawke for it. This was an example of a failed economic reform but, in comparison with the do-nothing Fraser period, the Hawke-Keating years did remove some of the long-standing irrationalities in the Australian economy and did so in the context of serious efforts to prevent budget blow-outs. To a large extent these trends continued in the Howard years but have largely stopped since that time.

Keating's greatest failure as an economic manager was the extraordinary rise in interest rates in the late 1980s when the cash rate reached 18 per cent in November 1989 and the standard variable mortgage rate 17 per cent, with many business loans over 20 per cent. In these circumstances it was quite a feat for the government to be re-elected, albeit narrowly, at the election in March 1990. In December 1991 Keating finally forced Hawke out of the party leadership, although by a very small margin in the final vote, to become Prime

Minister. All of these events are described by Bramston in meticulous detail so that the book is one of the most complete records available of Australian political history over the period of Keating's career.

In the election of March 1993 the government increased its share of the two-party-preferred vote and gained two seats. This was a rather remarkable result after ten years in office and appeared to be a product of the Liberals' GST proposal and, in a foretaste of the July 2016 election, doubts raised by Labor about the Liberals' commitment to Medicare.

This last period of government featured a number of Keating's agendas – engagement with Asia, movement towards a republic and legislative recognition of native title. But when the next election arrived in March 1996 the government had been in office for 13 years and the coalition received 53.6 per cent of the two-party-preferred vote – a landslide result in Australian terms.

Except perhaps for Whitlam, Keating seems to have struck the greatest chord with members and supporters of the Labor party amongst the leaders of the post-war years. His combination of passion, invective self-confidence and personal warmth made him an unusually attractive character to those on the Labor side of politics, although Hawke certainly had greater popularity in the general community. Bramston has skilfully captured this volatile mix of talents and produced a work that will remain the last word on its subject for a long time to come.

THE AUSTRALIAN

December 15-16, 2018

MCMAHON FINALLY ANSWERS THE CALL

Tiberius with a Telephone: The Life and Stories of William McMahon by Patrick Mullins

The conventional wisdom is that William McMahon was Australia's worst prime minister. In light of some of those who have occupied the office over the last decade, it must be doubted whether this can be true. Nevertheless, it is rather remarkable that he is the only prime minister who has not previously been the subject of a biography. That, at least, has now been remedied by Patrick Mullins' book.

McMahon was born in 1908 to parents of Irish and English descent. Because of his mother's illnesses and his father's seeming indifference, he and his three brothers spent most of their childhood with relatives or in boarding schools. Money, however, was never a problem as his grandfather had built up an enormous transport business and, when he died in 1914, his legacies ensured McMahon would never have financial problems during his lifetime. After law school at Sydney University, McMahon became a partner at the establishment firm of Allen, Allen & Hemsley and something of a minor playboy in Sydney's wealthy eastern suburbs.

McMahon was more interested in politics than law but both were put to one side from 1940 during the war years, which he spent as a staff officer, finishing as a major, on the home front. Immediately after the war he took up the study of economics at Sydney University. For the December 1949 federal election the House of Representatives was expanded from 74 to 121 seats so there was scope for newcomers and McMahon secured Liberal pre-selection for the electorate of Lowe in Sydney's inner west. The book provides plenty of detail on these early years of McMahon's life and is a graphic reminder of what a different Australia existed at that time.

McMahon was re-elected in the 1951 election after the original pre-selected Labor candidate, John Kerr, dropped out shortly before the poll. He became minister for navy and air, followed by social services and primary industry, entering the inner ministry or Cabinet in 1956. His colleagues regarded him even then as a relentless provider of government secrets to the media and the book recounts an incident where, after giving the material to a journalist on one day, he joined prime minister Menzies the next day in reprimanding the newspaper for irresponsible behaviour in publishing the information.

The chapters on McMahon's life and times are interspersed with the long-running account of how McMahon's proposed autobiography was pushed away by various publishers and caused despair in ghost writers who were confronted by 27 filing cabinets of documents. The author of this book did not have access to that material but it might be doubted whether this is such a disadvantage. He has certainly engaged in wide-ranging and meticulous research on his subject.

After the Labor split in 1955, the breakaway Democratic Labor Party ensured the continued election of the Menzies government. In 1958 McMahon became minister for labour and national service so that he presided over the system of conscription by ballot that was introduced in late 1964. 1965 was the year of Australia's troop commitment to the war in Vietnam and also the year that he married Sonia Hopkins, 24 years his junior and an extremely rich Sydney socialite. Some of his colleagues continued to marvel at McMahon's position as a senior minister but, as the book points out, he had the advantage of coming from New South Wales in a party to some extent dominated by Victorians and also the strong backing of Sir Frank Packer who owned Sydney's *Daily Telegraph*.

When Menzies retired in January 1966, Harold Holt became prime minister but, again to the surprise of some of his colleagues, McMahon was elected deputy leader of the Liberals by a narrow margin over Paul Hasluck. He became treasurer which resulted in a series of serious clashes with deputy prime minister and National Party leader, John McEwen, on tariff protection. The Holt government won a landslide victory at the 1966 election but was already showing signs of strain when Holt was drowned in December 1967. McMahon was vetoed as Holt's successor by McEwen but survived as deputy Liberal leader to the new prime minister, John Gorton. Hasluck said of this performance:

> In my limited experience I have never seen anything done with such brilliant cunning and today I think he is in a stronger position than he was the day before Harold died … in a wry sought of way I recognise McMahon now as being a more clever man than I thought he was, although my distrust of him is greater than ever and my contempt for his political methods is profound.

Under the leadership of Gough Whitlam, Labor was emerging from two decades of electoral exile but initially Gorton's rough charm struck a chord with the Australian public. This was not to last. His erratic and wilful style alienated many of his parliamentary colleagues and the premiers of the Liberal States. In 1971 he was ambushed by army minister, Malcolm Fraser, and resigned as prime minister. As the last man standing, McMahon took over. It was Whitlam who described the plotting McMahon as "Tiberius with a telephone", which Mullins uses as the title of this biography.

In retrospect, the election of the Whitlam government in December 1972 appears to have an air of inevitability. The Liberals had been in office for an unbroken period of 23 years and were riven with personal conflicts. Moreover, McMahon obviously lacked the eloquence and gravitas of Whitlam. Nevertheless, the election result was relatively close, with only five seats needed to have gone the other way. One factor in all this was a still reasonably strong vote for the DLP but the fact is that McMahon was defeated only rather narrowly.

Ironically, as the book details, many of the McMahon government's expenditure and regulatory initiatives were taken up and expanded by the Whitlam government. It is often forgotten that the Liberal governments of the 1950s and 1960s were no champions of small government. This book is an important and well overdue contribution to Australian political history.

AUSTRALIAN BOOK REVIEW

June-July 2019

CONSIDERING THE COMPANY I KEEP

A lucky and resilient prime minister

Robert Menzies: The Art of Politics by Troy Bramston

There have been at least half a dozen previous biographies of Robert Menzies but Troy Bramston's new life of Australia's longest-serving prime minister is arguably the most attractive combination of research and readability.

Menzies was born in 1894 in the Victorian country town of Jeparit. Its population was then only two hundred but Menzies did not have a deprived childhood. His father ran the general store and was later a member of the Victorian parliament. Menzies finished his school years at one of Melbourne's elite institutions and then attended law school at Melbourne University where he won many academic prizes and headed a wide range of student bodies.

His university years largely coincided with those of the Great War. His two elder brothers enlisted but, under family pressure, Menzies did not. This was a far-reaching decision, given the fact that in the 1920s and 1930s there was a real gulf in Australian society between those males who had fought in the war and those who had not done so.

Menzies started at the Victorian Bar in 1918, reading with Owen Dixon who would later become the High Court's Chief Justice, and taking silk in 1929 as the youngest King's Counsel in the country. He combined this extremely successful legal career with the world of politics, entering the Victorian parliament in 1928 and in 1932 becoming Attorney General and deputy premier in the United Australia Party state government. Not all of his political colleagues appreciated his wit. When accused in a parliamentary debate of having a superiority complex, Menzies replied: "Considering the company I keep in this place, it is hardly surprising."

In 1934 he moved to the federal political scene where he at once became the Commonwealth Attorney General and soon afterwards deputy to UAP prime minister, Joseph Lyons. Despite this meteoric rise, not everyone was an admirer. Victorian premier, Stanley Argyle said to one of Menzies' new federal colleagues: "Thank god we have got rid of him. You're welcome to him." Menzies resigned from the federal Cabinet in March 1939 but, when Lyons died a few weeks later, he returned as prime minister. As the book notes, when war broke out in September, Menzies still favoured negotiations with Hitler's Germany. So did many British politicians but Menzies was certainly blunt in a letter to Australia's high commissioner in London, saying that "nobody really cares a damn about Poland."

Britain suspended elections during the war years but political conflict in Australia continued largely unabated. The 1940 federal election did not produce a majority for any party but Menzies continued as prime minister, although he spent considerable amounts of time in London and seemed anxious to swap his Australian role for one in the British war Cabinet. This was not to be, however, and in August 1941 he was deposed by his own party. A few months later Labor took office under John Curtin.

This was certainly the low point of Menzies' career but, as the book explains in some detail, he worked tirelessly over the next few years to create the Liberal party from the ashes of the UAP, culminating in a decision to form the new party at a conference of community organisations in Canberra in October 1944. Labor won the 1946 federal election comfortably but lost office in 1949.

Menzies became and then remained prime minister from 1949 until 1966, although the book makes the often overlooked point that, like almost all successful politicians, he had some exceedingly good luck. The 1954 election was very close and the 1961 poll was decided by one seat. If those results had gone the other way, Menzies' career would have been quite different. Moreover, after the Labor split of 1955 the Liberals were able to rely on the preferences of the Democratic Labor Party which affectively kept them in office until 1972. And, after Chifley's death in 1951, he faced opposition leaders in Evatt and Caldwell who largely lacked electoral appeal.

It needs to be remembered that Menzies never led a conservative government. There was no notion of small government but a continuing increase in federal legislation and expenditure, symbolised by the rapid growth of Canberra and its bureaucracy. Nor was there any focus on economic reform with tariffs remaining substantial and industrial relations highly centralised.

On the international stage Menzies was not as sure-footed as he was at home. When Egypt, under the leadership of Colonel Nasser, nationalised the Suez canal in 1956, Menzies led a delegation to try to persuade Nasser to compromise. It is true that the Americans effectively torpedoed these negotiations but it was always a dangerous diplomatic exercise and his support for the British and French position also appeared to be misjudged when they invaded the canal zone but were soon forced into an ignominious withdrawal.

During the Menzies period Australian troops were sent overseas to fight in four conflicts: the Korean war in the early 1950s, the suppression of communist guerrillas in Malaya throughout the 1950s, Indonesian incursions into Borneo in the mid 1960s and Vietnam from the early 1960s. The last of these was far and away the most controversial decision in retrospect, although it was largely supported by the Australian community until it became clear towards the end of the 1960s that the war in Vietnam could not be won. The first significant commitment of Australian ground troops to Vietnam was made in April 1965 and, although the book is critical of this decision, it does not quite explain the full cynicism of Menzies and his Cabinet colleagues. It was obvious that they had no concern for South Vietnam or its people but it is now clear that they had no concern for the long-term interests of the United States either. The Australian commitment was designed to be an insurance policy with the Americans and Canberra was indifferent to the consequences for them if the war could not be prosecuted successfully. As it turned out, the war caused serious divisions within the American community and significantly damaged the international standing of the US, to some extent in a way that has never been repaired.

It was once conventional wisdom that Menzies dispatched his rivals, such as Percy Spender, Richard Casey and Garfield Barwick, to posts outside politics but, as the book makes clear, these were not really rivals in the first place. He did, however, leave something of a vacuum behind when he retired in early 1966. His long-term deputy Harold Holt, became prime minister but was struggling in this role when he was drowned in late 1967. John Gorton succeeded Holt but was deposed by his own party and William McMahon was defeated in the 1972 election.

Menzies health deteriorated in retirement and he died in 1978. This book details his remarkable career and is a very welcome addition to Australian political biography. I would, however, have omitted the entire chapter containing Menzies' – extremely bad – efforts at poetry.

THE RULE OF LAW
OR
THE RULE OF LAWYERS

Quite a number of these articles make the case against a bill of rights. This kind of regime has been instituted in Victoria, Queensland and the Australian Capital Territory and was close to being adopted at the national level during the period of the Gillard and Rudd governments. I have long argued that a bill of rights represents a transfer of power from elected parliamentarians to unelected judges and that legislation of this type deals not with legal issues but social, economic and political questions. One of the reasons for the bitter contests over appointments to the US Supreme Court in recent years is the recognition in that country that its bill of rights, enshrined in the Constitution, gives the court the decision-making power on many important political matters. Even the UK Supreme Court could not resist interfering in the political process in the contest over Brexit.

One other way in which economic and social questions have often been entrusted to lawyers in Australia is by the use of royal commissions. There may be occasions where an inquiry into a limited set of facts is justified but more often royal commissions represent a decision by governments to put off making policy in difficult areas. Moreover, they are a very costly and inefficient means of devising public policy, even if their recommendations are ultimately accepted, which in many cases they are not.

There is also some discussion of the law of defamation and contempt – two areas that raise important questions of freedom of speech and are, for that reason, of particular concern to the media.

THE RULE OF LAW
OR
THE RULE OF LAWYERS

AUSTRALIAN FINANCIAL REVIEW
24 February 1984

ROYAL COMMISSIONS … THEIR USE AND ABUSE

It was once suggested, based upon its proliferation at the national and State level, that Australians had a talent for bureaucracy. It might equally be argued that they have a talent – if that is the right word - for Royal Commissions.

Historically Royal Commissions have been at the heart of some of Australia's most dramatic political events. The Petrov Commission of 1954 is still the subject of fierce debate over whether it was engineered in part by Menzies to influence the election of that year. In the same way that the Petrov Commission helped to destroy Evatt as a political leader, the Mungana Commission of 1930 was largely responsible for preventing Theordore's accession to the Labor leadership.

Even in the darkest days of World War II, violent political controversy surrounded the Royal Commission set up to examine allegations that the Menzies-Fadden Governments had approved a defence plan that involved abandoning all the continent above the so-called Brisbane Line. And in the last 12 months the Hope Commission at the national level and the Street Commission in New South Wales have both commanded months of headlines as they examined issues that in each case had serious political implications for the governments concerned.

There are two basic models for Royal Commissions and these should be distinguished because it can be argued that their potential consequences are quite different. There may well be inquiries that have characteristics of both models or that cannot easily be fitted into either category but politically the distinction is crucial. The first model is the fact-finding body established in circumstances in which a government itself is disqualified from acting as the fact-finding entity. The normal reason for disqualification is that the interest of the government and/or individual ministers or departments would raise doubts in the community as to its own judgment of the situation.

The Street Commission, which was established in 1983 to examine allegations of interference with the administration of justice by the NSW Premier, Mr Wran, was a clear example of this model. This exercise can be contrasted with the request to Mr Justice Hope to examine the ASIS raid on the Melbourne Sheraton Hotel in November 1983. There appears no reason in this case why the relevant minister should not have obtained the facts from his own officers and decided what action to take. The minister had no involvement in the events in question and there was therefore no reason why he should not have been inquiring into them.

The second, and over the last decade rather more common, model is that of the Royal Commission as a wide-ranging canvas of mixed fact and policy questions resulting in a series of policy recommendations to the government of the day. The most significant feature of this model is that it involves the consideration of clearly political issues by the inquiring body and the making of recommendations on these questions that in practice governments find difficult to reject. Examples of this kind of inquiry would be the Ranger Inquiry presided over by Mr Justice Fox and conducted between 1975 and 1977 into the extremely sensitive political issue of uranium mining and export, the first Royal Commission on Intelligence and Security conducted between 1974 and 1977 by Mr Justice Hope and the current Royal Commission on the Use and Effects of Chemical Agents on Australian personnel in Vietnam established in May, 1983, with Mr

Justice Evatt as Commissioner.

The first model, the fact-finding exercise in which the government itself is not the most suitable body to undertake the inquiry, is obviously a legitimate use of Royal Commissions by governments, and there will continue to be occasions on which this kind of inquiry will have to be undertaken at the Federal and State level. The second model, the consideration of political questions and the making of policy recommendations, gives rise, however, to serious questions.

The overriding issue of principle on the second model is its basic incompatibility with the concept of responsible government. This concept suggest that ultimately decisions ought to be made by ministers as the representatives of the majority party elected to government. Everyone appreciates that in many cases those decisions are based upon the advice of the minister's department and/or outside advisors and community bodies.

It might seem, therefore, that the notion of Royal Commissions, being only the providers of recommendations, do not cut across this idea of government. In theory they do not but in practice the most significant aspect of Royal Commissions and many non-royal Commission inquiries is that they are conducted by a member of the judiciary. This has invested them with a status different from that of other advisory bodies in the minds both of politicians and the public. The result has been the effective substitution of unelected persons for politicians in the analysis of what are often highly contentious political questions.

There is another important objection to the use of judges. The point of the debate on the appointment of judges, most recently raised by Mr Justice Kirby in his Boyer Lecturers, is that the present system has, with a small number of exceptions, produced a judiciary in Australia of clearly-defined and homogeneous values. This is not the place for a debate on the worth of those values but it must be obvious that the common denominators of sex, background, working experiences and social circles among senior barristers, to whom the Bench has been essentially restricted, would produce a body of opinion that is strongly inclined to traditional conventional values.

Again, it must be stressed that this is not the time for a debate on those values. They are firmly held by certain sections of the community and are therefore entitled to an impact on the political process. But the problem of the use of the judiciary to consider economic, social and political issues by way of Royal Commissions is that these values have a quite disproportionate input into the political process. It is hardly necessary to add that the use of senior barristers, not yet appointed to the Bench but close to that appointment, is for these purposes the same as using a member of the judiciary.

There will be some discussion below of the manner in which Royal Commissions are conducted, but it should be noted here that the presence of a senior barrister instructing the judge sitting as commissioner, and of barristers and solicitors representing various parties with interests in the commission, are likely to reinforce those values that are already brought to the inquiry by the judge presiding over it. Further problems arise from the actual conduct of the inquiry. The Royal Commission form of inquiry, not surprisingly in view of the presence of a judge and counsel, often employs very largely the format of the courtroom. This entails oral submissions, examination-in-chief of witnesses by counsel assisting the commission and cross-examination of witnesses by the various interests represented before the commission. Whatever the merits of this system in the trial of a criminal or civil action it is fairly obviously unsuited to the consideration of policy issues.

The time taken to report by Royal Commissions is, of course, very closely linked to the question of format. The adoption of a courtroom format inevitably means a protracted exercise. Even when hearings have not been a significant factor, however, Royal Commissions have often been conducted over an inordinate time. Some of the longest running of the 1970s were the Royal Commission on the Petroleum Industry conducted by Mr Justice Collins (1973-1976), the Royal Commission into Drilling for petroleum on the Great Barrier Reef presided over by Mr Justice Wallace (1970-1974) and the Royal Commission on Human Relationships headed by Justice Elizabeth Evatt (1974-1978).

One consequence of the length of many Royal Commissions is that the final report, whatever its other value, is often received long after the political climate that inspired the establishment of the inquiry has changed. As a result there may well be little enthusiasm for the implementation of the commission's recommendations. In the case of a number of the commissions mentioned above the government that established them had departed before their reports were received.

The kinds of costs involved are indicted by the Royal Commission on the Activities of the Federated Ship Painters and Dockers Union, established in October, 1980, with Mr Frank Costigan, QC, as commissioner and continuing. Up to September, 1983, Mr Costigan had received $993,750 in fees and the two counsel assisting $668,950 and $406,232 respectively. These figures, which seem more relevant to budgetary items such as a hospital or a school than to an individual, are of course only part of the commission's cost. There is a support staff of more than 70 and the best estimate is that the commission had cost about $10 million up to the end of 1983.

What are the alternatives to Royal Commissions? One is obviously to rely more upon the existing machinery of government ie the departments and agencies that work in these policy areas all the time. In a situation where public debate is considered desirable, there is no reason why this could not be a two-stage process under which the relevant department or agency prepares a discussion paper, then final recommendations to the minister after reactions to that paper.

It may be, however, that a minister wants an outside assessment, because, for example, the relevant departments and agencies have conflicting interests on the issue in question or have traditionally taken a different view from that of the minister. In these circumstances it ought to be possible to establish a task force of three or five persons with relevant expertise and set a strict time limit for its report. It would not be necessary to have members of the judiciary in this role. Support staff would be required, but in the absence of the courtroom model written submissions by interested parties would be the norm and only limited provision would be made, if at all, for oral submissions.

There is nothing novel in this approach. Such bodies have operated in the past at the State and federal levels and are still doing so. They do not normally receive the same kind of publicity as a Royal Commission. But at every level the task force model is likely to be more efficient than the cumbersome Royal Commission. Like Dr Frankenstein's monster Royal Commissions are very easy to create, very difficult to stop and almost impossible to control.

THE SYDNEY MORNING HERALD
Tuesday, September 21, 2004

WHY TRIALS FOR WAR CRIMES COLLAPSE

The world needs a new form of tribunal to deal with the likes of Saddam Hussein

The trial of Slobodan Milosevic – which resumed recently – and the proposed trial of Saddam Hussein – as yet without a starting date – raise a real question as to how heads of government and other senior figures in deposed regimes should be dealt with.

In many cases, and certainly in the case of the former Serbian and Iraqi administrations, those regimes have been responsible for substantial loss of life in other countries and amongst their own people. In historical terms, however, the idea of dealing with this conduct by way of some kind of legal process is very recent. For centuries the leaders of the losing side were normally killed out of hand. The Nuremberg trials marked the beginning of what has become a common reaction to the large-scale loss of civilian lives in wars with neighbouring nations or in civil conflicts inside one country.

But it has become clear in recent times that the procedures used for domestic criminal cases cannot be easily translated into prosecutions for war crimes, genocide and crimes against humanity. In a trial on a charge for armed robbery, for example, there is likely to be an exhaustive examination of events to establish whether the accused person was directly involved in what occurred. If this approach is applied to a series of incidents in different parts of a country over a period of years, it is very difficult to bring the case to an end.

This has been illustrated by the trial of Milosevic. He is being tried before a United Nations tribunal in The Hague. There are sixty-six charges arising from the conflicts in Croatia, Bosnia and Kosovo between 1991 and 1999. So far the hearing has lasted more than two and a half years. All this time has been consumed by the prosecution case but, now that Milosevic has begun his defence, he says that he wants to call over 1,000 witnesses, including Tony Blair and Bill Clinton. The presiding judge, Sir Richard May, died earlier this year and has been replaced by a new member of the court.

The same problem eventually caused the UN tribunal in Rwanda to collapse under its own weight. It was set up to try the Hutu perpetrators of the massacre of 800,000 Tutsis in 1994. Although some cases were heard, most of the accused had to be released after years in prison waiting for trial and a process of reconciliation was substituted.

The Milosevic case also highlights one of the particular difficulties that arise when senior members of an administration are put on trial. It is usually impossible to find the smoking gun, that is, the direct order that the killing of civilians be carried out. This is hardly surprising. Even in the case of the highly bureaucratic system that the Germans instituted to kill six million Jews in the early 1940s, there were no instructions in those terms by the leaders of the regime, and least of all by Hitler himself.

All this suggests that a new form of trial is needed for those in the category of Saddam Hussein and Milosevic, whether it is carried out in an international tribunal or at the domestic level. There is no doubt, for example, that, while Saddam was head of government in Iraq, its forces invaded Kuwait and over decades also killed hundred of thousands of Iraqi citizens, in one case by the use of poison gas. Why cannot these facts be taken for granted and Saddam held responsible as the head of government without years of evidence as to chains of command and letters of authority? It is presumably too late for this course to be adopted at The Hague. But could it seriously be suggested that the massacres of Bosnian Muslims took place without the knowledge and approval of Milosevic?

It may be objected that this is "victors' justice". But, in many ways, this must always be so. Only the losers are ever prosecuted and, as at Nuremberg, one of the charges is likely to be waging a war that ought never have been started. It is important to remember that even this kind of hearing would never be granted if the situation were reversed. It is not difficult to imagine the fate of Churchill and Roosevelt if the Germans had been victorious in 1945.

It is important for the survivors of these crimes and for the families of those who have not survived to see the Saddams of the world put on trial. But there needs to be a better system than the one that has reduced the Milosevic proceedings to its present impasse after two and a half years of hearings.

THE AUSTRALIAN
Thursday, January 7, 2016

SOCIAL MEDIA ABUSE PUSHES DEFAMATION LAWS TO THE LIMIT

There is no easy way to balance freedom of speech and protection of reputation

It seems that the law of defamation has a bad reputation at the moment and there have been quite a number of calls for change. Many of these calls have suggested that the law is simply not equipped to deal with the explosion of social media publications over recent years.

The current legislation on this subject is a uniform statute that was adopted by all the States and both Territories in 2005 and came into effect on 1 January 2006. It was largely, although not entirely, based on the then existing law in New South Wales and was an attempt to strike a balance between the two competing values of freedom of speech and protection of individual reputation.

There is no easy solution to reconciling these two goals and litigation in this area has always been time-consuming and expensive, not least because the defendants are often large media organisations who can afford high-charging teams of lawyers.

There are, however, two changes that could be made to the existing legislation that would significantly reduce the volume of litigation. The first is the requirement – introduced into the UK defamation legislation in 2014 – that a publication must have caused or be likely to cause serious harm to the reputation of the plaintiff before there can be any liability for its dissemination. This would presumably have a chilling effect on trivial claims, although it might be noted that there are already some judgments of Australian courts that would allow these kinds of actions to be dismissed at the outset on the basis that the length and cost of the litigation would be completely disproportionate to any harm suffered to the plaintiff's reputation.

The other change that might also have a deterrent effect on defamation claims would be the introduction of what is known in the United States as the "public figure doctrine." Under American law so-called public figures – a notion that includes not only politicians and public office holders but also movie actors and sports stars – can only succeed in a defamation action if they establish malice on the part of the publisher. This could be demonstrated, for example, by a lack of honest belief in the truth of the publication by the journalist. But this could normally only be shown if the sources and information available to the journalist were so obviously unreliable that he or she could not have genuinely accepted them as accurate.

One of the rationales for this doctrine is that public figures have considerable access to the media and are able to defend themselves there against charges of improper conduct. This is not to say, however, that serious charges, such as bribery in the case of a politician, should be able to be made in the absence of apparently reliable information. If there was no such information, it can hardly be argued later that there was an honest belief in the truth of the allegation.

What about the problems created by publications on social media? It may be, of course, the first of the changes proposed – the requirement of serious harm to reputation before an action can be made out – might dispose of a sizable proportion of those claims based on items on social media. But, depending on the number of persons with access to them, some publications on social media have the capacity to be extremely damaging to a person's reputation. There cannot be any real solution to this problem until there is a greater realisation in the community that making an allegation against a named person on social media is no different to making the allegation on the front page of a national newspaper. In each case the publisher is exposed to exactly the same risk of liability.

One way in which the 2005 legislation did reduce an area of

defamation litigation was by banning actions by corporations except for non-profit bodies and small companies with less than ten employees. It might be thought that large corporations have staff whose sole function is to promote and publicise their activities and so are well-placed to respond to any allegations made against them. There was, however, considerable opposition to this provision and the business community would no doubt like to reopen the issue.

All this suggests that, while there is certainly a case to be made for some reforms to the existing legislation, there is no basis for dismantling it and starting again. There is no magic formula that will accommodate absolute freedom of speech and complete protection of reputation so there will always be a debate as to the proper balance to be struck by defamation law between these two poles.

THE AUSTRALIAN
Monday, March 28, 2016

US PROVIDES A SALUTARY LESSON ON POLITICISING JUDGES THROUGH A BILL OF RIGHTS

Elected representatives are more suited to reaching outcomes of contentious questions

Many Australians would be puzzled to observe that a recent vacancy on the US Supreme Court has set off a firestorm in American politics. The vacancy was caused by the death of Justice Antonin Scalia and will provoke a major confrontation between President Obama, who makes the nomination to fill the vacancy, and the Senate which has to approve the nomination under the US Constitution.

The Republicans have 54 of the 100 members of the Senate and so can block any nomination by the President if they vote together. It is true that in Australia the federal parliament does not need to approve appointments to the High Court which are made by the executive government. But it is also true that such appointments in this country are seldom matters of political controversy. Why is this different in the US?

The answer lies in the bill of rights that is part of the US Constitution. It has resulted in highly contentious political questions, such as capital punishment, abortion, gun control and funding of election campaigns, being decided not by the elected politicians in the Congress but by the Supreme Court. Naturally many members of the community have strong views on these kinds of issues and bitterly resent decisions of the court that find against their beliefs. These feelings are accentuated because they know that they have no say in the selection of the judges of the court in the same way that they do for members of the Congress.

The political nature of many of the court's decisions are reflected in the fact that over recent years the nine members of the court have often divided five votes to four on these kinds of questions. Four of the current judges are supposedly liberal and four supposedly conservative with one oscillating between the two groups. Justice Scalia was a member of the conservative group but it would normally be expected that president Obama would nominate a liberal lawyer to replace him. This would significantly alter the balance of power on the court and so has raised the stakes considerably for this nomination.

There have, of course, been frequent calls for a bill of rights at either the state or federal level – or both – in Australia. Both Victoria and the Australian Capital Territory already have a statutory bill of rights. The problem is, as the American experience demonstrates, that handing over political questions to courts does not turn them into legal questions. All it means is that political issues are determined by judges and not by elected parliamentarians. So what happens is the politicisation of the judiciary or, put another way, the judicialisation of politics.

There is, therefore, something fundamentally anti-democratic about a bill of rights but this has never been considered a valid objection by the academics, activists, and legal professional bodies who constantly call for this exercise. They think judges are better qualified than politicians to decide on social and economic policies for our society. So they positively welcome a transfer of power from the parliaments to the courts. It would be easy to be cynical and say that it is hardly surprising that many legal groups are in favour of legislation that is likely to generate substantial litigation and so serve the financial interests of the legal profession. But it is important to realise that the proponents of a bill of rights are in fact ideologically motivated and want political issues to be decided in the courts.

A bill of rights is in any event a self-defeating exercise because none of the so-called rights in the Victorian and ACT statutes are absolute. To take the example of freedom of speech, there have always been legitimate restrictions including the law of defamation, contempt of court and protection of national security. So a general reference to freedom of speech only invites argument about what the exceptions will be and this then becomes under a bill of rights a subjective exercise for the courts rather than the parliament.

The question that comes out of the conflict in Washington between the President and the Senate is whether we would want to see judges of the High Court politicised in the same way as judges of the US Supreme Court. If we don't, it will be necessary to resist the calls for a bill of rights in this country. If we are going to have arbiters of our society, better to elect them than to appoint them from the ranks of the legal profession.

THE AUSTRALIAN
Friday, July 22, 2016

BILL OF RIGHTS A PICNIC FOR LAWYERS, A BEGGAR'S BANQUET FOR DEMOCRACY

Queensland's government should stand firm against vested interests' push for new charter

The Queensland government has been invited to a lawyers' picnic. This carnival is to take the form of a bill or charter of rights to be enacted by the Queensland parliament.

In September 2015 the government announced that the Parliament Legal Affairs and Community Safety Committee would consider the question of whether Queensland should have a statutory bill of rights. Even before this announcement, however, the government had been deluged with submissions, following its taking office in February 2015, from legal academics, legal professional bodies and community law centres asking for the introduction of this kind of legislation. These groups blanketed the parliamentary committee with similar submissions.

Now the parliamentary committee has concluded its inquiry and its report was tabled in the Queensland parliament on 30 June. All government members recommended the introduction of a bill of rights and all Opposition members voted against this idea. The vacuous quality of the majority's views is reflected in its conclusion that: "Society is changing at a rapid rate and views are also changing in response. Consequentially there needs to be a mechanism which allows these to be addressed."

A cynic might say that, of course, many lawyers would be in favour of legislation that is likely to generate substantial litigation and so will serve the financial interests of the legal profession. A bill of rights does provide considerable work for lawyers but those groups who support its enactment actually have a strong belief that courts are better qualified than parliaments to decide the important questions in our society. They believe that a lot of economic, social and political questions would be better handled by judges than by elected politicians. They reject the notion that in a democracy these issues are ones for elected representatives rather than unelected judges. They seldom acknowledge publicly, however, that those issues do not become legal questions by being handed over to courts. They remain economic, social and political issues but ones that are now decided by courts instead of parliaments. It is very easy to point out the deficiencies of politicians but, as Winston Churchill was inclined to say, parliamentary democracy is the worst system of government except for all the others.

Victoria and the Australian Capital Territory already have a statutory charter of rights. These models demonstrate the limitations of any bill of rights. The Victorian charter, for example, says that every person has the right to "freedom of expression". There have always been a range of inhibitions in our society on freedom of expression, such as the laws of defamation, contempt and official secrecy. So what happens with a bill of rights is that this generalised freedom is then subject to any number of qualifications – but with the important difference that the extent of the qualifications is decided by the courts and not by parliaments.

In similarly bland fashion, the Victorian charter also provides for a "right to life", although without any reference to the questions of abortion or euthanasia. It would seem highly unsatisfactory that these contentious issues would be ones for the courts rather than for the political process. Many of the other rights set out in the charter appear somewhat academic, such as freedom from torture, freedom from slavery and freedom of movement within Victoria. Was there any suggestion that these freedoms were not universal in Victoria prior to the passage of the charter in 2006?

It is hard to see how litigation in the courts can be a useful solution to what are largely political questions but, as already noted, those in favour of the bill of rights see litigation as an easier way of bringing about changes in society than trying to convince governments to bring about those changes.

It would be nice to think that the Queensland government would reject the anti-democratic proposal put forward by the majority on the parliamentary committee but there is little in the way of countervailing forces in our society to the interest groups that relentlessly campaign for this transfer of power from parliaments to the courts. It is hard to see why a group of parliamentarians would engage in this form of suicidal behaviour but the most likely result from all this is a Queensland bill of rights with all the problems that come with this kind of legislation.

COURIER MAIL
Tuesday, November 8, 2016

SHOULD BIG DECISIONS BE LEFT TO OUR COURTS OR PARLIAMENTS?

Last week Premier Annastacia Palaszczuk announced Queensland was to have a bill of rights similar in form to the Victorian charter of rights. This follows an inquiry by a parliamentary committee that reported in June of this year. All government members of the committee recommended the introduction of the bill of rights and all opposition members voted against this proposal.

The key point of disagreement between proponents and opponents of a bill of rights arises from the fact that this kind of legislation represents a transfer of power from elected representatives in parliament to unelected judges in courts. Those against a bill of rights say that this is fundamentally anti-democratic. Those in favour believe that parliamentarians cannot be trusted in this area and that many economic, social and political questions would be better decided by judges. It is important to remember that political issues do not become legal issues if they are handed over to the courts. They remain political issues but ones that are now considered by judges. Opponents of a bill of rights do not suggest, of course, that judges should be elected. They simply say these matters should be left for elected members of parliament.

It is true that under the Victorian model the courts are not able to declare legislation invalid. They are, however, able to make a finding that a law is incompatible with the charter of rights. Arguably, there is little difference in practice between these two outcomes because it would be very difficult for a government to leave untouched a law that has been held by a judge to be contrary to human rights. In any event, both exercises require the courts to consider political rather than legal questions. In addition the charter allows an individual to sue a government body on the ground that it has acted in a way incompatible with one of the charter's rights.

The Victorian model illustrates many of the problems with bills of right. One of the rights it establishes is freedom of expression. This is an important value in our society but has always been subject to accepted restrictions, such as the law of defamation, contempt of court and protection of national security. So a general reference to freedom of expression only invites argument as to what the exceptions to it will be and these political questions then become a subjective exercise for the courts rather than for the legislature.

The Victorian charter also establishes a right to life, although there is no clue as to how this may affect legislation that authorises abortion or deals with the question of euthanasia. These are issues that can be the subject of strong views in the community and are hardly suitable for consideration by the courts.

Then there are a whole set of rights in the Victorian charter that appear to be largely academic in the context of Australian society. Consider, for example, the charter's establishment of the following rights: freedom from torture, freedom from slavery, freedom of religion and freedom of movement within Victoria. Is there any suggestion that these freedoms were in any danger before the passage of the charter in 2006? Is there any suggestion that they are in danger in Queensland today?

Many proponents of a bill of rights want to add to these kinds of freedoms a set of economic and social rights, for example, a right to affordable housing and to schools of a certain standard. Are these the kinds of questions that are suitable for decision by the courts rather than the parliament?

One other consequence of a bill of rights is that it inevitably encourages various individuals and groups in the community to see legal proceedings rather than political action as a way of achieving their agendas. It is often difficult to achieve social and economic change by exerting public pressure on politicians but that is how the Westminster system of government works. It should not be able to occur through the back door method of legal proceedings. It is also hard to see why anyone would want to encourage additional litigation, given the time and expense of any action in the courts.

In any public debate on whether Queensland should have a bill of rights it is important to remember that what is at stake is where decisions are made on a range of issues that are important to all members of the community.

SYDNEY MORNING HERALD
January 28-29, 2017

THE COURAGEOUS BARRISTER WHO PURSUED A LANDMARK VERDICT

Murder at Myall Creek: The trial that defined a nation by Mark Tedeschi

Mark Tedeschi QC is the Senior Crown Prosecutor for New South Wales but has found time to write a number of books on celebrated criminal cases. The pivot on which this new work turns is the notorious murder in 1838 by 12 stockmen of 28 aboriginal men, women and children camped peacefully on the Myall Creek station in northern New South Wales.

The book is, however, largely a biography of John Plunkett who prosecuted in the two trials of the killers. Plunkett was an Irish barrister who came to the colony of New South Wales in 1832 to take up the post of Solicitor General. As a Catholic, he only became eligible for such an appointment in 1829 when the British parliament removed most of the restrictions on members of that faith holding public office. In 1836 he became the colony's Attorney General but continued to carry out the duties of both positions. As the book explains, the colony was divided, often acrimoniously, between three groups – convicts, those who had been convicts but were now emancipated and those who thought themselves superior because they had never been either. One of the most powerful sections of the community was the so-called squatters who had established large pastoral holdings in the north of the colony, one result of which was the complete disruption of local aboriginal communities.

When the trial of the stockmen commenced, they had expensive defence counsel paid for by the local land owners from the Myall Creek area. Tedeschi is, of course, completely conversant with the workings of the criminal law in 1838 and explains that there could only be one victim in relation to any particular trial for murder, no matter how many accused had been charged. This presented problems of identification for the prosecution, particularly because one witness saw the aboriginals being led away and a different witness saw their largely burnt bodies.

Plunkett was the subject of considerable public criticism for initiating the prosecution and the first trial resulted in not guilty verdicts. But this was where the one victim rule played into Plunkett's hands. He chose a different victim for a second trial of seven of the stockmen who again made no statements on their own behalf. This time the verdict was guilty and, after an appeal was dismissed, all seven were hung, despite public petitions and violent editorials demanding that the sentences be commuted. It is something of an irony that Plunkett himself was opposed to capital punishment.

Shortly after these events there were major changes in the life of the colony with the end of transportation in 1840 and the first organs of responsible government in 1842. Plunkett assisted in drafting the 1842 legislation while in London and then returned to the colony to seek the office of Chief Justice. He was unsuccessful but continued to enjoy a wide-ranging public career. He remained Attorney General until 1856, presiding over many significant law reforms, including the introduction of civil marriage. He had terms in the Legislative Assembly and in the Legislative Council, where he was at one time President, before coming Attorney General once more in 1865. He was also one of the early Vice Chancellors of Sydney University after its establishment in 1850.

Plunkett emerges as a rather austere and at times difficult character from these pages but there was no lack of courage on his part, particularly in his pursuit of the Myall Creek murderers. He was an important character in early Australian history but has previously been little known, even to those interested in these times. This book fills a significant gap in the story of the infant colony, as well as being a reminder of one of the worst atrocities committed against the Aboriginal people during this period.

THE AUSTRALIAN
Monday, July 3, 2017

CRITICISM OF COURTS NOT ALWAYS CONTEMPT

The recent actions taken by the Victorian Supreme Court against three federal government ministers – and the *Australian* newspaper - in recent weeks raise the question of how the law of contempt strikes a balance between the administration of justice and freedom of speech. The ministers had commented on the court's sentencing of persons convicted of terrorism offences and the newspaper had reported those comments.

The law of contempt has more usually been invoked in the case of a criminal trial conducted with a jury. If, for example, a media organisation – or now a Facebook participant – published shortly before or during a jury trial that an accused person charged with sexual assault had been previously convicted of similar offences, this would very likely be a contempt because it might make the jury more disposed to convict the accused of the current charge.

It is important to note that a charge of contempt is itself a criminal prosecution that can result in a term of imprisonment or, in the case of a media organisation, a very substantial fine. This may be one reason why the law of contempt has been invoked much less often in the case of civil litigation as opposed to criminal trials. It is also true that juries have largely disappeared in the civil area, except for defamation cases, and the courts have always assumed, hardly surprisingly, that no judicial officer could be influenced by any kind of publication.

There are, however, several forms of contempt that may still be applicable to publications about civil or criminal proceedings that have not been concluded, even though they will be decided by judges without a jury. One of the best-known examples of this occurred in

1974 when a British newspaper, the *Sunday Times*, was found guilty of contempt in relation to a series of articles suggesting that the manufactures of the drug thalidomide had negligently caused serious birth defects and should not contest the claims for damages brought against them. One basis for the decision by the House of Lords was that the publications amounted to a prejudgment of the cases against the manufacturers or, more colloquially, "trial by media."

The Australian courts have been reluctant to uphold this ground of contempt and it may be that it is fallen into disuse in this country. That would be logical in view of the courts' assumption that judicial officers will not be influenced by these kinds of publications. But the Victorian Supreme Court expressed concern that, despite this assumption, the statements of the federal ministers were intended to influence the court in its sentencing of offenders for terrorism offences in a particular case still before it. In one sense this would be an attempt to do what the judges acknowledge to be impossible but conduct designed to interfere with the administration of justice has always been contempt.

The other basis for contempt raised by the Victorian judges was that of "scandalising the court". This ancient formula covers conduct that might undermine public confidence in the administration of justice. So in 1900 the editor of the *Birmingham Daily Argus* was found guilty of contempt for describing a judge as an "impudent little man in horse-hair, a microcosm of conceit and empty-headedness." There have, however, been few examples of this principle being applied in recent times, largely because it has been recognised that freedom of speech should allow what might be strong criticisms of court decisions once they have been made, for example, on the ground that the sentencing of particular offenders has been too heavy or too light. It would no doubt still be possible to commit the contempt of scandalising a court by such conduct as a false allegation that one of its judges had taken a bribe to decide a case in a particular way.

The importance, however, of freedom of speech in this area was pointed out by the English jurist, Lord Atkin, in a 1936 decision when he said: "But whether the authority and position of an individual judge, or the due administration of justice, is concerned, no wrong is committed by any member of the public who exercises the ordinary right of criticising in good faith, in private or public the public act done in the seat of justice .... Justice is not a cloistered virtue: she must be allowed to suffer the scrutiny and the respectful even though outspoken comments of ordinary men."

Ultimately the federal ministers' apology headed off any charges of contempt and meant that none of these issues had to be considered by the Victorian court. But the exercise is a reminder of the tensions inherent in the law of contempt between the values of freedom of speech and the proper administration of justice. This case should not be taken to suggest that there is any legal bar to expressions of opinion that amount to constructive criticism of the decisions of courts.

THE AUSTRALIAN
Monday, July 20, 2015

TOUGHER US DEFAMATION LAW MAKES IT HARD FOR PUBLIC FIGURES TO SUE

In light of the Hockey verdict, should the Australian law be changed?

In the wake of Joe Hockey's defamation verdict against the *Sydney Morning Herald* and the *Age,* there have been a range of calls for some aspects of the law of defamation to be changed. The current basis for defamation law in Australia is the 2005 legislation that is uniform in all the States and both Territories.

Most of these calls for reform are misconceived, although there is one important question that is raised by the Hockey case. The reason why most of those calling for change are under a misapprehension is that they appear to see the verdict as one based on the use of social media and think that the law of defamation is not designed to deal with this new phenomenon.

The basis for the $200000 verdict was a *Sydney Morning Herald* poster and two tweets emanating from the *Age* which used the words "Treasurer for Sale". These publications were separate from and did not include the full newspaper articles that were found by Justice White of the Federal Court not to be defamatory.

There is nothing new in an action based on a poster that does not contain the newspaper article that it is promoting. It may be that some of those persons who see the poster buy and read the newspaper but obviously some will not. The author Morris West, for example, successfully sued the Sydney *Daily Mirror* in the early 1970s over a billboard that referred to him. As for the *Age* tweets they were published by that media organisation and so it was responsible for their contents. The point about social media generally is that anyone who publishes defamatory material on, for example, Facebook, is liable to be sued if he or she can be identified and is amenable to the jurisdiction of the Australian courts. There may be many practical problems about bringing proceedings in relation to publications on social media but conceptually the law of defamation treats these publications in the same way as newspaper articles or television broadcasts and it does not need to be changed to deal with this new world of publications.

The one important question, however, that is raised by the Hockey case is whether Australian defamation law should be changed to reflect the American position where public figures can only succeed in a defamation action if they demonstrate malice on the part of the publisher. There may, of course, be some dispute in any particular case as to whether a person is a public figure but in normal circumstances this term would extend to politicians, holders of other major public offices, sporting stars and media personalities. Malice in this context is likely to be evidenced by a lack of belief of the truth of the publication or reckless indifference to whether it be true or false. This in turn leads to an examination of the journalist's sources of information and the quality of his or her research. The doctrine does not, therefore, mean that a politician or other public figure cannot recover in an action for defamation but it is certainly more difficult than under the Australian system. As it happens, the American model would not have helped the *Sydney Morning Herald* in the Hockey case because the court found that there was malice by reason of ill will towards Mr Hockey. But this is a relatively unusual finding so the media would normally be better off if there were a public figure defence.

There is a defence of statutory qualified privilege available under the Australian legislation for publications that, while false and defamatory, are made to provide information on subjects of public interest. But it is a further requirement of the defence that the conduct of the publisher is reasonable in the circumstances. This last requirement has proved extremely difficult for media organisations to establish in court proceedings.

Two of the factors that a court can take into account in looking at the issue of reasonability are the extent to which the publication is a matter of public interest and the extent to which it relates to the performance of the public functions or activities of the plaintiff. These two factors would seem on their face to allow some aspects of the American public figure doctrine to be used by Australian publishers in defending a defamation action but the record of the courts in this area is hardly promising for publishers and journalists. In these circumstances the introduction of a public figure defence would require legislative change and, as an important policy question, it is really a matter for the State and Territory parliaments rather than the courts.

THE AUSTRALIAN
Monday, July 30, 2018

TURNING JUDGES INTO POLITICIANS – THERE'S A BAD IDEA

The compromised US system proves why Australians need to be wary of a bill of rights

The announcement by US President Donald Trump of Brett Kavanaugh as a nominee to replace Anthony Kennedy on the US Supreme Court heralds a violent confrontation between Democrats and Republicans in the Senate, which has to approve the nomination. It is worth asking why appointments to Australia's High Court don't involve this kind of ferocious debate.

The difference lies in America's Bill of Rights which is contained in a series of amendments to the US Constitution. Like all such statutes, it transfers political decisions from the legislative body to the courts. That is why, for example, the circumstances in which women might have an abortion and the legality of same-sex marriage have been determined in the US not by the Congress or by State legislatures but by the Supreme Court.

One result of the court being in possession of this political power is that the judges of the court have essentially become politicians themselves. So in recent times the court has divided on contentious questions between four Republican judges and four Democrat judges with Justice Kennedy, although originally appointed by Republican president Reagan, providing the deciding vote. In the decision last month concerning bans on some persons entering the US from a number of countries linked with terrorism, Kennedy voted with the four Republicans and so provided a majority in support of the ban. This is the importance of Kennedy's replacement because, if president Trump's nominee is approved by the Senate, it can be assumed that the Republicans will enjoy a consistent 5-4 majority on the court.

It does not seem to be widely appreciated in Australia that all this was an important factor in president Trump's original election. Many of his voters understood that the Supreme Court makes highly political decisions and that the only way of influencing those decisions is to be able to make appointments to the court. At the time of the election there was a vacancy on the court following the death of Justice Scalia and the party that won the election would have the ability to fill this place on the court. As it happened, president Trump's nominee was approved by the Senate but it can be assumed that a very different nominee would have been proposed if Hillary Clinton had won the election. None of this was lost on many Republican voters.

Why then are legal professional bodies in Australia and so many of the country's legal academics insistent that there should be a bill of rights at the national level and in all States and Territories? Why would anyone want to inject judges into the political process in this way?

There are, of course, already bills of rights on the statute books in Victoria and the ACT and the present Queensland government has pledged to introduce one in that State. It might be said that neither the Victorian nor ACT Supreme Court suffers from the divisions of the US Supreme Court. But the Victorian and ACT legislation has been in operation little more than a decade. It has taken the US Supreme Court two centuries to get to its current rigid division between judges. It is true that, because of the Bill of Rights, there has always been the potential for political conflicts on the US Supreme Court and these were reflected, for example, in its decisions on some of president Roosevelt's New Deal legislation in the 1930s. But those divisions have never before been as stark as they are on the present court.

But Australian proponents of Bills of Rights are not disconcerted by this American precedent. They believe that judges are better qualified to make political, social and economic decisions than members of parliament. So some of them might be - but they have not been elected by the community and that has never been the role of the courts under the Westminster system. As Churchill said of the process of electing governments to make these kinds of decisions, it is the worst possible system except for all of the others.

Presumably most of the Australian supporters of Bills of Rights would not be in favour of a provision like the second amendment to the US Constitution which provides for a right to bear arms and has proven an obstacle to gun control legislation in America. But this is a good example of how the workings of legislative bodies can be frustrated by these kinds of statutes.

Many of these Australian supporters, however, want a bill of rights to deal not only with traditional political questions like freedom of speech but also with economic and social rights such as rights to affordable housing and to schools of a certain standard. Are these really the kinds of questions that are suitable for decision by courts rather than parliaments? It might seem unlikely but we could finish up with a worse model than the US and even greater politicisation of the courts.

THE AUSTRALIAN
Thursday, November 8, 2018

RIGHTS CHAMPIONS WINNING

These bills of rights transfer power from the parliament to an unelected judiciary

The introduction into Queensland parliament of the Human Rights Bill 2018 represents another triumph for the group of legal academics, legal professional bodies and community law centres that have worked unceasingly over the last twenty years for the enactment of this kind of legislation.

Like rust, these activists never rest. They succeeded in having human rights legislation adopted by the ACT parliament in 2004 and by the Victorian parliament in 2006. Queensland is now to follow suit and, assuming a change of government at the federal level early next year, lobbying will start at once for the introduction of a national bill of rights. This was close to happening during the Rudd-Gillard period but was thwarted by the opposition of number of persons on the Labor side, including former NSW Premier, Bob Carr.

The chief objection to these kinds of statutes is that they are essentially contrary to the Westminster system of parliamentary democracy. They are designed to transfer political questions from elected parliamentarians to unelected judges. Shifting political decisions from legislative bodies to courts does not convert them into legal questions. It simply means that political decisions are given to judicial officers.

This is why the contest over Justice Kavanaugh's appointment to the US Supreme Court was the subject of such ferocious conflict. The American bill of rights has resulted in many important political decisions, such as the right to abortion and the status of same-sex marriage, being decided by the Supreme Court and not by the

Congress. This makes appointments to the court enormously important to many members of the community on both sides of politics.

It is true that the Victorian and ACT bills of rights – and the proposed Queensland legislation – do not, unlike their American counterpart, allow courts to declare invalid statutes that are inconsistent with the charters of rights. But they do require the courts to construe legislation in accordance with the charters. They also allow the courts to declare any inconsistency between legislation and the charters and this obviously places considerable pressure on governments to change existing statutes or to avoid this happening in the first place.

None of these objections, however, would faze proponents of bills of rights. They want political, social and economic questions to be decided by the courts and not by parliamentarians. They consider that judges are better qualified to decide these questions, not least because they are not subject to pressure from uninformed members of the electorate as politicians are.

The more practical objection, however, to bills of rights in the Australian context is that they are simply unnecessary. Is there any suggestion that citizens of New South Wales enjoy less rights than the citizens of Victoria or the ACT who are supposedly protected by legislation in those jurisdictions? Or that the citizens of Queensland are currently disadvantaged in comparison with their opposite numbers in Victoria and the ACT?

There is no evidence that many of the freedoms nominated for protection by the Queensland Bill have ever been threatened by any government in this country. Is there any suggestion, for example, that it is necessary to legislate to protect the citizens of Queensland from torture, slavery or restrictions on their movement in and out of the State?

Even in the case of more conventional freedoms, such as freedom of expression, all that bills of rights, including the Queensland model, do is to provide that this exists. Freedom of expression exists without legislative endorsement but has always been subject to a range of qualifications, such as the law of defamation, which protects reputation, the law of contempt, which protects the administration of justice, and laws safeguarding national security. It is then left to the courts to say how many qualifications there will be to a freedom that is phrased so generally as to be almost meaningless.

Many proponents of bills of rights are not content to have only such traditional notions as freedom of expression enshrined in legislation. They also want to include what they describe as economic and social rights and the Queensland Bill includes a right to education and a right to health services. It might be thought that these questions are budgetary decisions for governments and not a suitable subject for litigation in the courts which were never established to deal with these kinds of issues.

Naturally there is scope under the Queensland Bill for complaints to be made to the Queensland Human Rights Commission. This is essentially the same model as exists for the federal Human Rights Commission that has allowed defendants to essentially trivial complaints to be the subject of lengthy and expensive legal proceedings over a number of years.

The great paradox of bills of rights is that by defining rights and freedoms they at once confine them. In the absence of legal restraint, there is a general freedom of action in our society. What's wrong with leaving that alone?

THE AUSTRALIAN
Thursday, September 26, 2019

JUDGES TRUMP VOTERS

Around the world, the judiciary is having too much say in politics

This week's decision of Britain's Supreme Court that suspending the parliament was unlawful is an extraordinary contribution to a long-term trend in Western countries – the judicialisation of politics, that is, the transfer of political, social and economic issues from elected governments to unelected judges.

The decision to prorogue or suspend the British parliament, for a matter of weeks only in this case, was no doubt made for the same reason that all government decisions are ultimately made – to assist the ruling party in its political agenda. There is no question here of misleading the Queen because she is obliged to act on such a request from her current ministers. But this is exactly the kind of question that has traditionally been considered outside the realm of judicial review, chiefly because governments are accountable to the electorate and not to the courts for their political decisions. If the electorate disapproves of a government action, it can demonstrate that disapproval at the next election.

It is, of course, possible to abuse the power of prorogation by using it to stop a vote of no-confidence in the government. But that is not what happened here. The government would welcome a vote of no-confidence so that it could go to an election. But the opposition groups in the parliament, while refusing to pass the government's legislation, have not been prepared to have these questions resolved by the electorate.

It is important to note that political, social and economic questions do not become legal questions when there are transferred to courts.

They retain their original character but are decided by judges and not by politicians. This is, of course, the whole point of a bill of rights which is designed to take issues like freedom of speech and even the availability of housing and education from governments and place them in the hands of the courts. Proponents of bills of rights cheerfully acknowledge this because they believe that judges are better qualified than politicians to make these sorts of decisions, despite the obvious inconsistency with democratic political theory.

The long-term results of leaving political questions to the courts is reflected in the current role of the US Supreme Court which determines questions like the availability of abortion and the validity of same-sex marriage under the bill of rights enshrined in the US Constitution. The current court is split 5-4 on Republican–Democrat lines and votes accordingly on all major issues that come before it. The confirmation of appointments to the court by the Senate has become a process of fierce confrontation between the two parties. In addition, the ability to appoint judges to the court has become an important issue in presidential elections and was one reason for president Trump's narrow victory in 2016.

It is significant that the decision of the UK Supreme Court was one of four judicial considerations of the prorogation challenge - by two Scottish courts and two English courts. Two of those courts, one Scottish and one English, rejected the challenge on the ground that it was a political and not a legal question. Naturally the UK Supreme Court has had the final word but all this illustrates the fact that this issue is far from clear and in those circumstances it might be thought that the courts would err on the side of caution and decline to become involved in the political process, as two of them did.

What next? Does this mean the courts can review the date on which an election is to be held or the appointment and removal of ministers? Whatever the merits of the decision to prorogue the parliament in this case, this was ultimately a question for the approval or disapproval of the electorate and not for the UK Supreme Court which has made a dangerous intrusion into the political arena.

The result of the 2016 referendum was never accepted by many powerful forces in Britain and one of their tactics to stop Brexit has been a series of court cases. Regrettably, in this instance, their anti-democratic conduct has been rewarded.

FRIENDS AND ENEMIES IN FOREIGN AFFAIRS

Most of these selections make a case for realism in the conduct of foreign affairs, both by Australia and by its long-time American ally. They accept that working relationships with other nations can exist, however unattractive some of their regimes and leaders might be. This is particularly so in the case of Russia where the West has been reluctant to accept that, as a major power, it cannot be prevented from maintaining spheres of influence around its borders and is bound to resent encroachments by NATO on those neighbouring zones. There has been an element of hysteria over recent years in Washington about Russian influence and, to some extent, in Canberra about the influence of China in this country.

The US foreign policy establishment has always been ready to enmesh American forces in the affairs of other countries. It was unsuccessful in achieving major intervention in what was a civil war in Syria, although it maintained the objective of destabilising the administration in Venezuela in an attempt to have it removed.

A number of these pieces are about the question of borders – how open they should be in the context of immigration, legal and illegal, and whether they should be redrawn if one province or region of an existing nation is determined on secession from the rest of the country.

FRIENDS AND ENEMIES IN FOREIGN AFFAIRS

THE AUSTRALIAN

Tuesday, February 19 2008

BIRTH OF A NATION DEPENDS ON LUCK

Kosovo's secession appears to have succeeded because the circumstances were propitious

The declaration of independence by Kosovo this week raises big questions about the notion of secession – the ability of a province or region in an established state to split away and have a separate legal existence. Throughout history this has been a source of enormous political and military conflict.

Kosovo was, of course, part of Yugoslavia until that nation's break-up in the 1980s. It then became a province of Serbia, although the great majority of its inhabitants are Albanian and not Serbian. This anomaly was – like many others in the Balkans – the product of centuries of conflicts over territory and constantly shifting boundaries.

The United States, Britain and France are expected to recognise Kosovo very quickly, despite the existence of a UN Security Counsel resolution that acknowledges it to be a sovereign part of Serbia. The EU is also supportive and plans to send in a large group of officials to replace the UN administration that has supervised Kosovo's affairs for the last ten years. The principal opponent of independence for Kosovo – except, of course, for Serbia – is Russia which can block further UN participation in the territory because of the veto it holds as a permanent member of the Security Council.

Historically one part of a state has been able to succeed only if it has been able to establish its separate existence by force of arms, either alone or with the assistance of sympathetic foreign countries. One of the greatest conflicts of modern history – the American Civil War – resulted from the – ultimately unsuccessful – attempt by a number of southern States to leave the Union. Ironically the Union had its origins in the successful breakaway from British rule by the original thirteen American colonies, although it is very doubtful that this would have occurred without the military support that they received from France at that time.

More recently attempts at succession have met with both success and failure. Biafra's efforts to break away from Nigeria in the late 1960s, failed after several years of civil war. Bangladesh – formerly East Pakistan – achieved independence in the early 1970s but only after India intervened to stop mass killings by the Pakistani government. Eritrea finally forced the Ethiopian regime to recognise it as a separate entity in the early 1990s, although border hostilities still simmer. Chechnya's attempt to leave the Russian federation has been, however, brutally suppressed over the last decade without a hint of criticism from the international community, which wished to maintain good relations with Russia.

What is interesting about the United Nations proposal for Kosovo is that it formally accepts the partial dismemberment of an established state, in this case Serbia. There is no doubt that the great majority of the inhabitants of Kosovo do not wish to be part of Serbia, although there is a Serbian minority who certainly do not wish to be part of an independent Kosovo. There is also a real issue as to whether Kosovo has the political institutions or economic resources to operate as a separate entity without continuing external assistance on a large scale. It has a population of only two million, although this is about the same size of Macedonia and Slovenia and larger than Montenegro.

Its economy, however, is extremely weak in comparison with these neighbouring countries.

But the really difficult question is how is Kosovo different from, for example, the Tamil region in northern Sri Lanka which has been conducting a war against the Sri Lankan government for many years. Or the eastern provinces of Bolivia which want to develop their natural resources without interference from the government in La Paz. Once the principle of secession is accepted, it is hard to say why one group in a particular country should be supported but not another in a different part of the world.

The answer in this case is that the Albanians in Kosovo have been lucky. Because their chief opponent was Slobodan Milosevic their cause was taken up by the NATO countries and used as a basis for dislodging the Serbian regime then in power. Now the international community has to deal with the results of the NATO victory and – except for Russia and, of course, Serbia – it is likely to do so, either sooner or later, by recognising Kosovo as a new state. Unlike many other attempts at secession, this one has succeeded, largely because of the alienation of the United States and the EU by Milosevic in the late 1990s.

THE AUSTRALIAN

Friday, September 30, 2013

WHY INTERVENE IN SYRIA?

A global superclass lacks roots in particular nations

Now that the prospect of US military intervention in Syria appears, at least for the moment, to have receded, the question arises as to who, inside and outside the Obama administration, was pushing for this highly unpopular proposal.

There was obviously little support for intervention in any broader community. In America, it may have been narrowly endorsed by the Senate Foreign Relations Committee but seemed to be struggling for approval in the House of Representatives. After the idea was rejected by the British House of Commons the only real support at the international level came, strangely given their history of opposition to American interventions, from the French government.

So, why Syria, and why now? Historically nation states have always been very reluctant to interfere with the internal affairs of countries that pose no threat to them. And yet the practice of justifying invasions on the basis that a population is being mistreated has been common since ancient times. For example, while there was no hint of a suggestion amongst the nations of Europe in the mid 1930s that they might take action against Germany because of its murder of any opponents of Hitler's regime or its brutal treatment of its Jewish community, Germany itself justified its annexation of the Sudetenland in Czechoslovakia in 1938 on the grounds that ethnic Germans in that country needed protection.

This might lead one to say, with Yeats, that the best lack all conviction, while the worst are full of passionate intensity, but the point to grasp is that it has never been taken for granted that nations have a right to interfere in other nations' internal affairs, no matter what the circumstances.

Sometimes, as in the case of Germany in the 1930s, such detachment means accepting terrible consequences for part of the local population. More modern instances of mass murder by a government against sections of its own people include Rwanda in the early 1990s and Pakistan's actions in the early 1970s in what later became Bangladesh. One of the reasons, of course, why nations have been so cautious about intervention in the internal affairs of their counterparts is that this kind of action creates an obvious precedent. If it can be justified in the case of a neighbour, it can be justified in the case of oneself.

Questions of intervention have always been decided on a more or less arbitrary basis. Are the deaths of many members of the Muslim Brotherhood in Egypt sufficient grounds for intervention from outside against the Egyptian regime? Seemingly not, because there seems to be no push for this. Nor did anyone suggest trying to forecibly restrain Russia's brutal quelling of the Chechnyan rebels in the 1990s. Russia is simply too powerful for there to be any notion of interference with its internal policies.

Which brings us back to Syria, where the Obama administration allowed its rhetoric to steadily reduce its available options. On its face Syria is an unpromising subject for outside involvement. The conflict there is essentially a tribal one. On one side is the Alawite regime of President Assad which is tolerant of various religious minorities, including Christians, who know what their fate would be if the rebels succeed. It is supported at the regional level by Iran and at the international level by Russia. On the other side are the Sunni forces, with a significant al-Qaeda component, largely funded by Saudi Arabia and Qatar.

However unattractive the Assad administration may seem, the real question for those in the West arguing for intervention is what kind of regime would take its place if it were removed. For while the Obama administration has insisted throughout that it only means to punish the Assad regime and so deter it from using chemical weapons again, surely it would have to be removed to ensure this end. At best, the success of the rebels would produce a government that was more hostile to the West and a less certain element in the volatile cocktail of hatreds that makes up the Middle East. At worst, a new regime might provide a base for terrorist activity and be a seriously destabilising factor in the politics of the region.

Why then did the Obama administration press for intervention? The crucial factor seems to have been the presence within the administration and the influence exerted on it by members of what could be called the international foreign policy and legal establishment.

This global "superclass" – diplomats, lawyers, and the occasional businessperson who spend their lives in transit from one conference to the next – lacks roots in particular nations. Often educated in multiple countries, their loyalty tends to be to be abstract ideas of international governance embodied in the UN, the EU, and the system of international treaties, rather than to their country of birth. While European and American pacifists in the war-ravaged nineteenth and twentieth centuries dreamed of such a class, it may be that the reality is not as good for peace as they hoped.

Free from the scourge of nationalist chauvinism these people may be, but they also do not have to face the consequences of the policies they recommend. They do not, unlike Congressmen and members of the House of Commons, have to face elections (tellingly, neither does President Obama, now in his second and final term). They do not have to supervise or witness first hand military operations, which are always performed by one or other national military force. They can therefore recommend war more easily than could a politician with a special regard for the interests of a single nation.

THE AUSTRALIAN

Tuesday, July 29, 2014

SCOTLAND CHIPS AWAY AT THE ENGLISH EMPIRE

The secession bid highlights the weakening cultural capital of one of the great powers

The referendum on independence for Scotland that will take place on 18 September has not had much coverage in Australia. But it is significant and it tells us more about England than it does about Scotland. Irrespective of the result, the fact that the referendum is being held at all underlines the decline of English culture and confidence over the last half century.

Historically there have been many provinces or regions in countries wishing to secede and become independent states. The most costly attempt at secession was made by the Confederate states of the Union in 1861 and resulted in a civil war that cost over 600,000 lives. The Confederacy might have succeeded with outside help. This was how Kosovo was able to split off from Serbia. Its independence was effectively recognised by the West in 2008, although still not by the Serbians, but this was a product of earlier bombing of Belgrade by NATO airpower. Bangladesh, formerly East Pakistan, achieved statehood in 1971 only after India used its military strength to force the Pakistani government to agree.

No such help was available to the Tamils in Sri Lanka or the Chechnyans in their conflict with the Russian Federation. The Crimea was able to rely on Russian protection to separate from the Ukraine and ignore Western protest. Several European nations face strong secessionist movements in one region of the country, including Spain in relation to Catalonia and Italy with its largely German-speaking far northwest province.

But the common feature in all these attempts at secession, whether successful or unsuccessful, has been that they were strongly opposed by the central government of the undivided entity. In the case of the Scottish referendum this is an exercise that has been approved and arranged by the current British government, even though it has the potential to undo a union going back more than 300 years to 1707. What self-respecting nation would not only allow but actually facilitate the possible dismemberment of a centuries-old bond in such a cavalier fashion? And the most bizarre aspect of the referendum is that the vast majority of the population of the United Kingdom will not have a vote. The vote will be confined to "residents" of Scotland, although it has just over eight percent of the UK population, including citizens of other EU countries. So Poles and Bulgarians will have a vote but expatriate Scots and most citizens of the UK will not.

There has been considerable discussion in Britain as to whether Scotland can survive as a separate economic entity. This debate does not, of course, go to the big question of why the referendum is occurring in the first place. It is, however, hard to imagine that an independent Scotland would not encounter severe economic problems. It is sparsely populated with, except for North Sea oil, limited physical resources. This is not to deny the commercial and cultural contribution that Scots have made to the UK and to countries like Australia, Canada and the US over a number of centuries. But amongst the consequences of independence would be the lapsing of the existing currency union and the removal of the Bank of England as a lender of last resort.

Even if the referendum fails, Scotland is likely to be granted further quasi-independence by the British government with more key functions being transferred from London. This devolution of powers in the UK has gathered pace over the last two decades not only in the case of Scotland but also in relation to Northern Ireland in order to accommodate the IRA gunmen who now sit in its Cabinet.

There are countries, like Australia and the US, that could not avoid a federal structure because they started as a union of separate states and those states would not surrender all of their existing powers. The price of union in those cases has been a degree of duplication of functions and consequent inefficiencies together with endless debates about who imposes taxes and who spends that revenue. It is hard to see, however, why a nation that does not have this kind of federal system would want to consciously move towards it. But this is what has happened in the UK under both the previous Labour government and the current Tory administration.

All these seem a long way from the heyday of Empire. There is a sense in which Britain never recovered from the Great War and this is underlined, in the year of the centenary of that conflict, by its allowing a referendum that would dissolve the existing union between Scotland and the rest of the UK. Whatever the result of the referendum, it marks another step on the decline of one of the great powers of the 18th and 19th centuries.

THE AUSTRALIAN

Friday, September 12, 2014

REGRETTABLY WAR HAS ALWAYS BEEN WITH US

Calls for the West to intervene in Syria and Ukraine reveal a lack of realism

Listening to many "experts" on foreign affairs and international relations over recent months, you may be forgiven for thinking that the world is witnessing events without any parallel in recent history.

Barack Obama's national address yesterday, although chiefly concerned with Islamic State activities in Iraq, was in many ways provoked by criticisms at home and abroad of current US foreign policies. One criticism has focused on a failure to take stronger measures to stem the loss of life and flood of refugees arising out of the conflict in Syria. There are however, two points to note in relation to events in Syria. The first is that the Assad regime is facing an insurrection that, if successful, would result in the deaths of all members of the regime and probably also many members of the Alawite group across the country. In these circumstances it is hardly surprising that the regime is fighting to the bitter end.

The second point to note is that, although the conflict has been particularly brutal on both sides, the spectacle of a government killing large numbers of its own people is far from unusual in modern times. Without canvassing the merits of the disputes, recent examples include the suppression of the Tamil insurgency by the Sri Lankan government, the conduct over many years of the regime in Myanmar, and numerous cases in African states. Almost everyone deplores the loss of life in these instances but the question of when intervention by other countries would be justified is a difficult one and, as it happens, intervention did not occur in any of these conflicts.

The other major source of criticism for the Obama administration has been the conflict in Ukraine. President Putin is a singularly unattractive character but his lack of charm should not lead observers to ignore the political realities of this situation. Because of its geographic location, Ukraine falls naturally within the Russian sphere of influence and was formally part of the Soviet Union and the old Russian Empire. There is traditional and significant division between its western and eastern segments with the latter having strong links with Russia. In these circumstances the overthrow of an elected pro-Russian government and the adoption by its successor of policies hostile to Russia was bound to result in some form of conflict. Nor has the Western policy of incorporating Ukraine into NATO helped.

The West does not have to approve of Russian conduct in relation to the Ukraine but it does need to recognise that in the long run it cannot prevent that country being part of the Russian sphere of influence. The use of economic sanctions to try to force Russia to temper its policies in this region may have some effect, although historically such measures have seldom worked, particularly in the case of great powers that are able to absorb considerable financial hardship without facing internal collapse. In any event, there is something artificial about a discussion of sanctions in circumstances where Russia supplies one third of the natural gas used by the European Community. This fact is scarcely mentioned because the Community cannot do without the gas and Russia cannot do without the revenue that results from its supply.

The lack of realism reflected in calls for action on the part of the West in relation to Syria and the Ukraine is in part a product of the rise of a class of international bureaucrats and human rights lawyers who consider themselves citizens of the world. They often hold passports from one or more countries but owe their allegiance to none, seeing themselves as agents of a global community that is entitled to intervene in the affairs of nation states whenever the governments of those states engage in policies with which they disagree. Most of Obama's closest advisers on foreign affairs belong to this group, although so far he has shown considerable caution in resisting demands for US intervention in a range of foreign conflicts. Some of these demands have, of course, also come from a number of Republican senators and congressmen in Washington, placing them in an apparently unlikely alliance with the citizens of the world.

What both groups have in common is a belief in the moral superiority of the West and its ability to shape history in a way it has never been shaped before (the "global community" that citizens of the world like to invoke really only consists of the US and the EU). "History is over," is the implicit slogan of both the hawks and the citizens of the world; the struggle between great powers and rival conceptions of the good life has supposedly given way to a new and permanent liberal world order in which force, for the hawks, and law, for the citizens of the world, will prevent any regression. But the world is what it is, and history isn't coming to an end any time soon.

THE AUSTRALIAN

Tuesday, December 27, 2016

WE PROVOKE THE RUSSIANS YET PANDER TO THE CHINESE

Why is Western diplomacy inclined to such double standards?

Why is there such a difference between Russia and China in Western eyes?

Both are great powers, inferior only to the United States in global terms and motivated - like all nations large and small - largely by some understanding of self-interest. For Australia, of course, China is a major trading partner and so there is an obvious reason to remain on good terms with the Chinese administration. But the natural tension between nations does not seem to warrant the position of studied hostility to Russia that has been a consistent aspect of the rhetoric of Australia and other Western countries in recent years.

It is not necessary to find Mr Putin attractive to accept that Russia has an obvious sphere of influence in relation to its regional neighbours. On this basis Russia would be unlikely to tolerate a regime seriously hostile to it in the Ukraine, with which it shares a border. It is hardly surprising that Russia resented Western support for the overthrow of the elected Ukrainian government in 2014 and its replacement with an administration that sought closer ties with NATO and the European Union. The US would - quite rightly - resent a hostile neighbour in its own region and this accounts for its acrimonious relationship with Cuba over more than 50 years, despite a thaw in very recent times.

Russia's annexation of the Ukrainian territory of Crimea in 2014 has been heavily criticised in the West but it has to be noted that the Crimea had been part of Russia for more than two centuries before it became part of the newly independent Ukraine in 1991. It had long been identified with major events of Russia's history, as illustrated by the Crimean war of the 1850s, and evidence suggests that the overwhelming majority of Crimean residents favour union with Russia.

It is true, of course, that Russia has intervened on the side of the Assad regime in the civil war that has been conducted in Syria over recent years. The wisdom as well as justice of intervention in Middle East conflicts by outsiders might certainly be questioned but, from a Western perspective, the survival of the existing, secular administration, however unpalatable in many ways, is probably preferable to its replacement by its equally violent and theocratic opponents.

How is any of this conduct significantly different from the great power actions of China, or, for that matter, from those of the United States? As we have seen recently in relation to the congratulatory phone call to president-elect Trump from his Taiwanese counterpart, China refuses to recognise Taiwan as an independent state and insists that it is simply one of its provinces, despite its existence as a separate entity since the late 1940s. Then there is the case of Tibet which was annexed by China in 1951. The Chinese crushed a rebellion against their rule there in 1959.

More recently China has asserted jurisdiction over the South China Sea, dismissing the claims of a number of other nations. In July of this year a United Nations arbitration tribunal rejected the Chinese claim but this ruling was simply dismissed by the Chinese who indicated that they intended to ignore it.

Both the Russian and Chinese regimes could, of course, be fairly described as authoritarian, although rather less is heard about China's policies in this regard than about repression by the Putin regime. Why, then, such a difference in Western opinion, especially when China is a much more obvious threat to the West's global dominance? One reason is that Russia presents itself as an alternative to the West in the global "culture war" in a way China does not. Hysterical claims that Russia "hacked" the recent US election aside - claims which tap into a long history of Russophobia in the West - the Russians did not mind letting it be known that they may have had a hand in the leaking of material damaging to Hillary Clinton. The Chinese, on the other hand, tread more carefully, quietly using their economic power to influence Western foreign and domestic politics.

None of this is meant to suggest that China should be the subject of an aggressive foreign policy on the part of Australia or any other Western nation, but only that both Russia and China should be treated as self-interested great powers who act like great powers in their own regions and do not welcome moral lectures from the rest of the world. Relatively few nations share the values of the West but all these countries need to be dealt with in diplomatic and trading relationships. This kind of realism in international relations may seem unattractive to many people but nations cannot afford the luxury of the likes and dislikes that individuals can indulge in.

THE AUSTRALIAN

Thursday, January 12, 2017

US SHOULD PUT THOUGHTS OF A NEW COLD WAR ON ICE

There are bigger fish to fry than hacks and Crimea

Who wants to restart the Cold War?

Almost thirty years after the end of this period of confrontation, itself lasting forty years, between the West and the Soviet Union, there seems to be a desire amongst some members of Congress in Washington to reignite this old conflict with what is now the Russian Federation.

The immediate pretext for this outbreak of hostility on the part of a number of Senators and members of the House of Representatives is an alleged campaign by Russia to influence the result of the American presidential election last November. The chief allegation is that the Russians hacked into the emails of a number of Democratic Party officials and distributed them to WikiLeaks who released them generally.

Several things might be noted about this allegation. The first is that, while it may ultimately turn out to be true, it could not be verified by the various US intelligence agencies – the CIA, the FBI and the National Security Agency – who investigated it. Their report said that they had "high confidence" – except for the NSA which only had "moderate confidence" – that the hacking had occurred but they adduced no evidence to support this finding. Second, no one has suggested that the emails were not genuine or that there is usually any problem about the publication of embarrassing material from inside a political party. Third, no one has seriously suggested that the publication of the emails had the slightest impact on the result of the presidential election.

The report of the intelligence agencies also stated that the Russians had organised critical comments about the Clinton campaign on social media platforms. If true, this may be unattractive conduct but scarcely the stuff of diplomatic break-down between two great powers. It is not surprising that the Russians did not want Clinton to win the presidency, given some of the hostility directed against them by the Obama administration and Clinton herself.

None of this is to argue that interference by one country in the elections of another is a good idea. But it can hardly be a basis for criticism by the Americans who have interfered in countless elections in other countries over the post-war years. To cite just one example, in the 1948 Italian elections the CIA, alarmed by the prospect of a Communist victory, showered money on Christian Democrat politicians, newspaper editors and trade union officials. Some of the money was privately raised in New York gentlemen's clubs to which many members of the CIA in those days belonged. Whatever the effect of this avalanche of cash, the Communists did not win the election.

The Russian role – or lack of it – in November's presidential election is, of course, a storm in a teacup. But it is symptom of the larger problem that some politicians in the West, most particularly in Washington, seem anxious to manufacture a dispute with Russia over questions in which the West has no real interest. Chief amongst these questions is the government of Ukraine. Russian shares a border with Ukraine and, as a great power, could hardly be expected to tolerate a hostile regime in that country. What was the interest of Western nations in supporting the removal of the elected Ukrainian government in 2014 and its replacement with the current administration? Did anyone in the West suggest at the time that this was a shocking interference in the internal affairs of another country?

There was initially criticism in the West of Russia's annexation of Crimea in 2014 but this has become muted in face of opinion polls showing over-whelming support for union with Russia within Crimea. Syria is not on the borders of Russia and raises different issues. Russia has essentially intervened on the side of the existing regime of president Assad whereas the United States has provided some support for the regime's opponents. It is far from clear, however, why it would be in the interests of the West for an admittedly brutal regime that is, however, not especially hostile to the West to be replaced by one that is at least as brutal and would probably be more hostile to the West.

The Cold War was largely a product of the Second World War that left eastern Europe under the control of the Soviet Union. This all ended in the early 1990s and it is not necessary to like everything about Russia or anything about Mr Putin to realise that Western attitudes to Russia should be determined by contemporary interests and not by out-dated historical enmities.

THE AUSTRALIAN

Tuesday, July 11, 12017

WHY THIS FRENZY AGAINST RUSSIA?

There is no excuse for the Cold War-style Russophobia that has gripped the West

America's ambassador to the UN, Nikki Haley, said recently "We will never trust Russia". As a general principle of international relations, not trusting *anyone* is probably a wise position but what is the particular problem about Russia?

This is a country that poses no military or political threat to the West. Yet the hysterical tone of some politicians in Washington and much of the US media generally is reminiscent of the worst periods of the Cold War. James Clapper, Director of National Intelligence in the Obama administration and currently at the Australian National University, has said that Watergate pales in comparison to the allegations about the Trump administration's links to Russia. It is something of an irony that over the Cold War years the left in most Western countries were still sympathetic to what was then the Soviet Union, despite the millions killed by Stalin's regime in the 1930s and 1940s. Now, however, Russia appears to have no friends on either side of politics in the West.

It is true, of course, that Mr Putin's administration is not particularly attractive to Western eyes, although it is no more autocratic then many others around the world, including China whom no-one wants to offend for economic reasons. Critics of Russia complain about its annexation of Crimea from Ukraine and its support for pro-Russian groups in eastern Ukraine. Neither criticism, however, acknowledges the political reality that Russia is still a great power, although not as significant as the US and China. Crimea had been part of Russia for centuries and was inevitably going to return to it. Does no one remember that the Tsar's summer palace was located at Yalta in the Crimea? Ukraine lies on one of its borders and it could never comfortably tolerate a hostile regime in a neighbouring country, which is what emerged in Ukraine after the West supported the overthrow of the elected government there in 2014.

The most puzzling aspect of this outbreak of Russophobia in Washington is the seeming premise of the various investigations and Congressional hearings that there is something illegal or improper about discussions between members of the Trump administration – before or after taking office – and Russian diplomats and officials. In the absence of a declared war between the two nations, why should this be a problem? Presumably officials in all US administrations and in all campaign teams leading up to an election have always met with representatives of numerous foreign countries. So why is the FBI conducting an investigation into this question and why are various Congressional committees examining it? The media and some members of Congress continue, however, to refer to "Russian contacts" as if this was somehow treasonous conduct but without ever explaining how this could be so.

Whatever the content of the disputed conversation between president Trump and former FBI director, James Comey, it is hard to see that it matters who is right when the subject matter was a pointless investigation into discussions between Russian officials and former national security advisor, Michael Flynn.

There is one separate issue that might be the subject of legitimate investigation – an allegation of Russian interference in the American presidential election by distributing emails illegally obtained from the Democrat campaign organisation. This may turn out to be true. It is hardly surprising that Russia would prefer a Trump administration to one presided over by Hillary Clinton, given the sanctions imposed on Russia over the Obama years. It might be noted, however, that an investigation by US intelligence agencies was unable to establish it as a fact. Three further points can be made about this allegation. First, no-one could seriously suggest that it affected the election result in any way. Second, the emails were genuine and normally the media welcomes the leaking of secret communications. Chelsea Manning and Edward Snowden have become heroes in many quarters for their boxcar disclosures of classified material. Third, all governments have preferences in foreign elections and none more so than the US which has funded political campaigns in other countries on numerous occasions over the post-war period.

One example of the interest of governments in foreign elections is the recent reporting of donations to the major parties in Australia from individuals supposedly associated with the Chinese government. It is not entirely clear why this is such a sinister exercise. As already noted, governments often have an interest in the future policy decisions of their counterparts in other countries. There may be an argument for banning or restricting the size of all political donations, domestic and foreign, but that is a large question and would, in any event, be subject to constitutional challenge in the High Court. At any rate, the Russians must be relieved that, just this once, someone else is the target of hysteria.

THE AUSTRALIAN

Tuesday, November 21, 2017

THE PRAVDA SEEMS TO BE THAT RUSSIA PLAYED NO ROLE IN THE US ELECTION

Allegations of the Kremlin's interference in the democratic process are nothing new

The seemingly endless saga about Russian influence in the last US presidential election has some echoes in the British general election of 1924.

The first Labour government, under prime minister Ramsay MacDonald, had been in office for 10 months, supported by, although not in coalition with, the Liberals after none of the major parties had secured a majority at the last election. In October 1924, however, the Liberals and Conservatives combined to bring down the government on the floor of the House of Commons and a fresh election was called. During the campaign the press published what was described as a "letter" from Grigori Zinoviev, President of the Communist International in Moscow, to the British representative on the Comintern Executive. The letter, amongst other things, called on the British Communist Party to set up revolutionary cells in military units and munitions factories. The press complained bitterly that the government had a copy of the letter but had not revealed it and had not made a proper protest to Moscow.

The letter was, of course, a forgery, concocted by a group of Russian émigrés. It was, however, a constant issue in the election campaign after which the Conservatives finished with more than two thirds of the seats in the House of Commons. An early example of hysteria over supposed Russian interference in another country's domestic affairs.

Moving back to present day Washington, there can be no doubt that the Putin administration would have preferred almost any candidate to Hillary Clinton, given her anti-Russian stances when she was Secretary of State. But what did the Russians do to act on this attitude? The original allegation was that they improperly obtained and released, through WikiLeaks, a series of embarrassing emails from the Democrat campaign headquarters. This allegation may be true, although investigations by various US intelligence agencies were unable to establish its truth with certainty. If it is true, it would obviously constitute an unwarranted, if not at all unusual, interference in the electoral affairs of another country, although it might be thought a little difficult for the Americans to complain about this, given their own interference in scores of foreign elections in the post-war years by way of financial and administrative support for various parties in those elections.

A second allegation now seems to be made – that the Russians posted material hostile to the Clinton campaign on social media. The answer to this allegation would appear to be so what! The whole point about social media is that it is open to any domestic or foreign person to publicise their enthusiasms and prejudices, although the impact of all this on voters in small towns in Wisconsin and Nebraska might be doubted.

As to the issue of contacts between the Trump campaign and Russian officials, it can be assumed that representatives of all major foreign nations maintained contact with the staff of both the Trump and Clinton campaigns. It would be remarkable if they did not. If any of those campaign staff engaged in illegal financial dealings with foreign entities or individuals or acted as foreign agents without being registered under the relevant legislation, they can be the subject of prosecution. But none of this seems to have anything to do with the result of the election.

Special Counsel Robert Mueller has so far brought charges against three persons associated with the Trump campaign but none of those charges relate to alleged Russian interference in the election. It may be that there will be further charges at some time but it is worth noting that months of intensive investigation by a large team of high level lawyers has to date produced no compelling public evidence of significant Russian involvement in the election campaign.

Ironically the only substantiated allegation in all of this is that the Clinton campaign paid a great deal of money for a dossier on Trump that they hoped would show he had engaged in conduct that would open him to the danger of blackmail by the Russians. Like the Zinoviev letter, however, the dossier turned out to be a fabrication and the Clinton campaign got nothing for its money. Clinton defended this exercise as "opposition research", although she would presumably not have been amused if a similar document had been prepared on herself.

It is getting on to 100 years since the British election of 1924 but there is still something about Russia that brings out fantasies and inspires a decided lack of scepticism in the Western media. As already noted, something might yet emerge about Russian interference, however ineffectual, in the last presidential campaign but, more than a year after election day, there has been a great deal of smoke but so far a distinct absence of fire.

THE AUSTRALIAN

Friday, February 9, 2018

IT'S NOT SMART TO REHEAT THE COLD WAR

Like the rest of us, Russia and China are looking after their own interests

Who wants to go back 20 years to the Cold War? The answer seems to be some highly-placed officials in Washington and London, although their counterparts in Canberra are sensibly more reluctant to join this exercise in belligerent nostalgia.

At the end of last year president Trump spoke of Russia and China as rivals that sought to "challenge American power, influence, and interests." Shortly afterwards US Defence Secretary, James Mattis suggested that great power rivalry posed a greater threat to American security than international terrorism. At the same time Britain's Chief of the General Staff, Sir Nicholas Carter, called for greater British defence spending on the basis that "we may not have a choice about conflict with Russia." And *The Economist* warned in late January: "If America allows China and Russia to establish regional hegemonies, either consciously or because its politics are too dysfunctional to muster a response, it will have given them a green light to pursue their interests by brute force. When that was last tried, the result was the first world war."

These faintly hysterical declarations suggest a complete lack of understanding of several centuries of modern history. Great powers, like the US, China and – still in many ways - Russia, have always pursued their economic and cultural interests quite aggressively and, in particular, have been unwilling to tolerate outside interference in their own immediate spheres of influence. This was why the installation of Soviet weapons just off the American coast produced the Cuban missile crisis of 1962 and why, as part of the agreement that those missiles would be removed, the US agreed to withdraw some of its own from a Turkish installation close to the borders of the Soviet Union.

There have been Western complaints about China's restrictions on navigation in the South China Sea but, whatever the issues of international law involved, this is an obvious sphere of Chinese influence. Similarly, it is hardly surprising that Russia resents Western interference in the administration of a country on its very borders in the form of Ukraine. It might be remembered that the elected Ukrainian government was toppled by a coup in 2014 to widespread Western approval and following the expenditure of $5 billion in Ukraine by the US in support of opposition political forces to the government.

Much of the responsibility for hostility between Russia and the West lies with president Clinton who in 1994 approved the decision to expand the NATO alliance into the Russian sphere of influence. That decision led to Hungry and Poland joining NATO in 1999 and then Bulgaria, Romania and the Baltic states of Estonia, Latvia and Lithuania in 2004. The veteran US diplomat and Soviet expert, George Kennan, had written in 1997 that: "Expanding NATO would be the most fateful error of American policy in the entire post-cold-war era" and that such a decision might be expected "to restore the atmosphere of the cold war to East-West relations." Kennan's warning was, however, ignored in Washington and the capitals of Europe.

Neither China nor Russia have engaged in any efforts to impinge upon America's sphere of influence even though this extends well beyond its neighbouring regions as far as Western Europe. In these circumstances it is hard to see any basis for the inflammatory rhetoric coming out of Washington and London about superpower rivalry. Naturally there will be competition between the US, China and Russia for economic advantage and political influence in unaligned areas like Africa, the Middle East and Central Asia but this has been true for decades. It is also true that many Western politicians appear to be puzzled and unhappy that neither China nor Russia have adopted the values of democracy, human rights and the rule of law. It is not that these values are completely absent in China and Russia but they are certainly very much subservient to the interests in the state. And neither of these superpowers welcomes moral lecturers from the West on their deficiencies in this regard.

None of this means that the Russian or Chinese regimes should be immune from criticism or that they need to be held up as models of public administration. But international relations is not – and never has been – about such likes and dislikes. It is about the realities of world power and some of the recent statements emanating from Washington and London seem to ignore the history of great power relationships. As already noted, however, Canberra appears to be more conscious of all this and, particularly in the light of Australia's economic dependence on China, understandably so.

THE AUSTRALIAN

Wednesday, March 28, 2018

LIKE A COLD WAR RUN BY HOTHEADS

The West is getting overexcited by Russia and China and it is time we calmed down

There is a note of collective hysteria in the decision this week by several Western countries, including Australia, to expel a selection of Russian diplomats. The generally overwrought attitude in recent times to Russia, and to a lesser extent China, has been likened to the days of the Cold War. But it is actually more irrational than the climate of fear generated in much of the West about those two nations in the 1950s and 1960s.

It is not necessary to like or admire the present regimes in Russia and China, authoritarian as they obviously are, although Russia somewhat less so than China. But it would be useful to inject a note of realism into relations with those regimes at the international level.

At the height of the Cold War, the Soviet Union and the US contemplated the possibility of mutually-assured nuclear destruction and came dangerously close to this outcome in the Cuban missile crisis of October 1962. In retrospect it is reasonably clear that Russia did not want to extend its dominion beyond its Eastern European satellites but that was not accepted by many in Western Europe and Washington at the time. Meanwhile China was considered a threatening presence in Asia, partly because of its support for North Vietnam in its conflict with the South and partly because of its exclusion from much of international relations as a result of non-recognition by the US. Again in retrospect it is clear that Hanoi was not acting as a proxy for China in the Vietnam conflict but had very much its own agenda.

In the absence now of any military threat posed by Russia or China, current concerns in the West appear to be based on Russian and Chinese insistence on a traditional sphere of influence and supposed attempts to interfere in the domestic politics of other countries.

Taking the first of these concerns, there is little point in complaining about the influence that great powers wish to exert in their neighbouring regions. It is hardly surprising, therefore, that China has an interest in navigation in the South China Sea, although this does not appear to pose a real problem for vessels of other countries. Similarly, Russia has an obvious interest in the government of Ukraine and was naturally offended when a regime friendly to Moscow was ousted by an effective coup in 2014 with considerable moral support from the West.

In relation to the question of interference in domestic politics, there has been some rather sensational coverage in the Australian media of donations to political parties by individuals associated with the Chinese regime and Chinese investment in particular sectors of Australian economy, particularly real estate. It might be thought that there is a problem about large political donations from domestic as well as foreign sources but the federal government has proposed legislation to limit donations by non-residents. As for the question of Chinese investment, free trade theory, which Australia is supposed to believe in, would suggest that foreign investment and business enterprises can be regulated in Australia in the same way as are domestic commercial entities.

Allegations of Russian interference in the politics of other countries began with the leaking of emails from the Democrat National Committee during the last US presidential election campaign. Evidence for this allegation may eventually be found but so far none has been produced. The same is true for any so-called "collusion" between Russian officials and the Trump campaign. The word "collusion" has a sinister connotation but it is hard to see that there is any problem about contacts between foreign diplomats and bureaucrats with presidential campaign staff. Presumably all foreign officials would see this as part of their job. To date the only charges against American citizens arising out of Robert Mueller's lengthy and exhaustive investigation have been for lying to the investigators about business dealings unrelated to the campaign. There have been charges against what are described as Russian trolls who are said to have placed fictitious items on Facebook, as no doubt did many American residents in a similarly futile attempt to influence the election result.

This leaves, of course, the attempted murder in England of Sergei Skripal and his daughter. It may be that this can be sheeted home to agents of the Russian administration, although this has not been possible to date. Skripal sold his country's secrets to foreigners and in this murky world there would be various groups with an interest in removing him. If agents of the Russian state were involved, diplomatic measures against Russia would be justified but there is yet no verdict on this question.

All of this, however, suggests that the recent fevered reaction to Russia and China in various parts of the West needs some sober reflection. Neither poses a military or political threat and, in the case of China, it is one of Australia's chief trading partners. A dose of realism rather than emotion is much to be preferred in international relations.

THE AUSTRALIAN

Friday, March 8, 2019

MADURO'S MISRULE IS NO EXCUSE TO FORCE REGIME CHANGE IN VENEZUELA

By taking sovereignty too lightly we step into a minefield of international relations

The campaign by the US and many of its allies to remove the government led by Venezuelan President Nicolas Maduro raises an important question in international relations – in what circumstances, if any, should a national government be forced out of office by external influence where it is not engaged in armed conflict with those seeking its overthrow.

There is no doubt that the current regime in Venezuela, like its predecessor under president Hugo Chavez, is a study in incompetence and has squandered the country's substantial revenue from oil production. It is hardly tolerant of dissenting opinions, although the opposition forces have been able to conduct large-scale public rallies without disruption and these events have been recorded by the international media. Nevertheless the US and a sizeable group of European and Latin American countries, along with Australia, have supported sanctions against the present regime and have formally recognised the president of the Venezuelan national assembly, Juan Guaido, as acting president of the country in place of Maduro.

When a country makes war on its neighbours and loses, it is obviously likely that its regime will be removed by the victorious powers and a new administration substituted, often one conducted by those powers for a period of time. But it has been relatively rare over the period of modern history for a national government to be displaced in any other circumstances, no matter how oppressive they may be the treatment of its own citizens. As an example, it would be hard to think of a more oppressive regime than North Korea during the post-war years. The plight of its own people was exemplified by a famine in the 1990s that resulted in the deaths of somewhere between a quarter of a million and 400,000 of its inhabitants. It is true that North Korea has been the subject of sanctions designed to deter its nuclear weapons program but there has never been any suggestion that outside forces would intervene and remove its long-standing regime. An even more dramatic example was the conduct of the Rwandan government that encouraged and allowed the killing of between half a million and one million of its own people in 1994. The government was overthrown by invading rebel forces in the aftermath of the killings but neither major outside powers nor the United Nations intervened while the massacres were taking place.

One of the few instances where a national government has been deposed by outside forces, if only in respect of part of its territory, occurred in 1999 when Serbian control of its province of Kosovo was deposed by a NATO campaign of aerial bombing of Serbian regions. Although part of Serbia, Kosovo had an Albanian majority who wanted independence and Western intervention brought this about. Another example from the post-war years took place in 1971 when India intervened militarily in what was then East Pakistan to halt a campaign of terror by the Pakistani government against its political opponents in this part of the country. The result of the Indian intervention was the establishment of the independent nation of Bangladesh. The US invasions of Granada in 1983 and Iraq in 2003 also resulted in the removal of the existing regimes.

But the problem in international relations with the forced removal of established regimes, however unattractive they may be to some members of the global community, is that this notion can be easily extended to a whole range of countries. Why not, for example, intervene in Myanmar to stop its government's persecution of the country's Rohingya minority that has resulted in almost three quarters of a million from that group fleeing to Bangladesh? No one has suggested that such a course of action occur. Nor has anyone proposed action against Spain to stop the trials of the Catalan separatists that will take place soon. Why should the Kosovans have their own country separate from Serbia but not the Catalans one separate from Spain?

National sovereignty is a principle at the heart of international relations and there is a danger in treating it too lightly. The Venezuelan people would almost certainly be better off under a different regime but there is a real question whether that should be achieved from inside or outside their borders.

THE AUSTRALIAN

Wednesday, July 17, 2019

OPEN BORDERS INVITE CHAOS

Nations must maintain orderly migration laws

"What kind of monsters put children in cages?"

It's a familiar placard among demonstrators opposed to US attempts to deal with the waves of intending migrants still arriving this week at its southern border from countries in Central America. The latest move by the US is a tough new asylum rule: migrants passing through a third country on their way to the US must first apply for refugee status there.

The friction on both sides reflects the tension in many Western countries between the desire of governments to maintain orderly migration, against a view that borders should be thrown open.

There is a problem of terminology here, given that those moving towards the US from Central America and to Europe from North Africa and the Middle East are commonly described as refugees or alyssum-seekers. The fact is that almost all of them are potentially illegal immigrants. This is not to criticise them for seeking a different and what they hope to be a better life in a Western country but it recognises a reality that has been obscured by references to the 1951 Geneva convention on the status of refugees.

The convention provided that a refugee was a person who had left his or her country because of a well-founded view of being persecuted in that country by reason of race, religion, nationality, membership of a particular social group or political opinion. In many ways, however, the convention has been overtaken by events in the course of the last decade. There are, of course, still persons in some countries who could fall within the convention's category of refugees, such as the Rohingya people in Myanmar and the Uyghur people in China. But no-one in 1951 really envisaged a situation where millions of individuals who were not the subject of persecution decided to leave their own countries and move to one with better economic opportunities and a generally higher standard of living.

It is hardly surprising that these mass movements have produced alarm in many governments and the communities of nations that are the destination of these intending immigrants. This was a contentious issue at the 2016 presidential election in the US and the status of illegal immigrants, euphemistically known as undocumented immigrants in that country, remains a source of vigorous political debate. Within the European Union Chancellor Merkel's decision in 2015 to effectively open the borders of Germany provoked a strong reaction from a number of EU members, including Poland, Hungry and Italy, who have refused to accept directions from Brussels on this question.

In Australia the unauthorised arrival of people by boat has been the subject of much political controversy over a long period of time. Boat arrivals have been largely halted, although unauthorised arrivals by plane still remain high. The Australian experience of such entries demonstrates one of the problems with the 1951 convention. Once inside a country it is easy to claim refugee status and this claim can then result in years of legal proceedings during which time the claimant will not be deported. If an application for refugee status is refused by the Department of Home Affairs, there can be an appeal to the federal Administrative Appeals Tribunal and in some circumstances then to the Federal Circuit Court and finally to the Federal Court of Australia. The time and expense involved in this litigation is reflected in the number of cases that immigration matters occupy in the federal judicial system.

Most Western countries, including Australia, have a system for authorised immigration and also an annual quota of refugees who are taken in. Those refugee advocates in all countries who criticise this kind of system seem to offer no alternative to it other than a notion of open borders. How could this work when there are potentially millions of people in Africa and the Middle East who would like to live in the West? Australia is an island continent and so could exercise some control over entry but Europe and the United States do not enjoy this advantage.

Historically one of the characteristics of any nation was that it exercised control over its own borders. There is no obvious alternative to governments maintaining this long-standing position even in the face of the dramatic changes to population movements that have taken place over the last decade.

THE AUSTRALIAN

Tuesday, October 22, 2019

TRUMP WILL NOT PLAY BY THE RULES OF THE FOREIGN POLICY ESTABLISHMENT

They are powerful, dedicated opponents of the President – so he just ignores them

There is plenty of room for disagreement about the merits of Donald Trump's presidency but his decision to withdraw American troops, relatively small in number though they were, from Northern Syria is an important symbol. This is because it underlines his challenge to the dominance exerted over America's international relations in the post-war years by the north-eastern foreign policy establishment.

This is a group that sees American interests in every corner of the globe and has been prepared to promote those imagined interests with the presence of US troops on the ground in many cases. It consists of a mix of politicians, State Department bureaucrats, some journalists, much of the intelligence community and various think tanks. The paradigm of this approach to foreign policy was Vietnam where the US spent two decades of blood and treasure before leaving in defeat.

It should be noted that the foreign policy establishment has over the post-war period been a largely bi-partisan group, with its membership consisting of both Democrats and Republicans, although weighted more heavily to Democrats because of their electoral control of most of the north-eastern States where the group has its base.

In its constant search for enemies this group has in recent years focused particularly on Russia and China. In the Cold War years Russia did pose a military threat to the West but this is in the past. As a great power, although not as great as the US and China, Russia is realistically entitled to a sphere of influence over its immediate region. This includes Ukraine and particularly the Crimea which was part of Russia until its accidental attachment to Ukraine at the dissolution of the Soviet Union. The sanctions instituted by the West against Russia over its 2014 annexation of Crimea are futile, because the annexation will not be reversed, as well as damaging to both sides. Russia's hostile reaction to the expansion of NATO in the 1990s up to its borders was quite predictable and, for that reason, opposed by George Kennan and other students of Russian history.

As for China, it must also be expected to act as a great power in its own region, which is one reason for the West not to become over-excited about Chinese territorial claims in the South China Sea. China's economic influence seems to be of particular concern in some sectors in Washington – and in Canberra – but it needs to be remembered that Chinese investment in other countries, including Australia, is then subject to the domestic policies and regulation of those countries. It does not really help this debate to say that China is under Communist party rule, given that the party is only the vehicle for the kind of autocratic regime that exists in many parts of the world.

It is important, however, not to overstate Trump's challenge to the foreign policy establishment. Washington's efforts to remove the existing regime in Venezuela, for example, is an old-fashioned case of interference in a domestic administration that does not involve any obvious US interests. But Trump has never been part of the foreign policy establishment and that has always caused alarm in its ranks. It is no coincidence that from the outset his presidency has been undermined by material leaked by members of the intelligence services and this is the source of the current impeachment investigation undertaken by the House of Representatives.

In fairness to Barack Obama, it must be recognised that he spent much of his presidency resisting calls for the US to intervene militarily on a large scale in what was essentially a civil war in Syria. As a result, he faced the same kinds of criticism that Trump is now attracting over the withdrawal of the limited force that was posted to one part of Syria.

America's sixth president, John Quincy Adams, advised that his country "goes not abroad in search of monsters to destroy." Otherwise, he said, the nation "would involve itself beyond the power of extraction, in all the wars of interest and intrigue, of individual avarice, envy and ambition, which assume the colours and usurp the standard of freedom." Adams gave this advice in 1821 but it has never been accepted by many of the foreign policy makers in the US since that time. And Donald Trump will continue to find the current members of the foreign policy establishment constant critics and dedicated opponents.

THE AUSTRALIAN

Friday, January 3, 2020

SO WHO NEEDS NATO?

The threats it was created to counter passed long ago

The North Atlantic Treaty Organisation has just celebrated its 70th anniversary, having been established in 1949 with 12 member countries, mostly from Western Europe, including Britain and France, but also extending to the United States and Canada. Since then the membership has expanded to 29 countries, with five additional nations keen to join, including Georgia and Ukraine.

At the height at the Cold War, during the 1950s and 1960s, NATO's chief role was as a deterrent to any possible attack on Western Europe by the Soviet Union and its various satellites in Eastern Europe that constituted the Warsaw Pact. Following the disintegration of the Soviet Union and the collapse of the Warsaw Pact in the late 1980s and early 1990s, almost all of those former Soviet satellites ultimately became members of NATO.

It is very doubtful that the Soviet Union, either before or after the death of Stalin in 1953, ever seriously contemplated an invasion of Western Europe. The Soviets, and particularly Stalin, were adamant that the countries of Eastern Europe should remain under their control, if only as a buffer against the kind of German advance eastwards that had occurred during the Great War and then most dramatically in June 1941 with the invasion of the Soviet Union. But there is little evidence that the Soviet leaders considered expanding beyond those satellite nations, although they did, of course, act swiftly to maintain their control of those countries when it was challenged in Hungary in 1956 and Czechoslovakia in 1968.

At any rate, whatever threat Russia posed in the Cold War years, it hardly poses a physical threat to Western - or Eastern Europe - at this time and has not done so since the early 1990s. It is true that Russia annexed the Crimea in 2014 but this did not demonstrate any general territorial ambitions. It is possible to have a debate about the historical status of Crimea, given that it was once and for a very lengthy period part of Russia. But, whatever the merits of that dispute, it is obviously a special case and its annexation cannot sensibly be regarded as evidence of Russian designs on the countries of Europe.

This raises the question of what is the present purpose that is served by NATO. It is no doubt attractive to the Europeans to have some sort of guarantee of assistance from the US in a crisis but it is hard to imagine where a real threat to their security might come from. The two great threats to Europe over the last century came from Germany and it can be assumed that there will not be a repetition of those events. Nor can China – the other great super power after the US – be considered a danger to Europe in any kind of military sense.

It might be said that, even if it represents no threat, Russia is still hostile to the West. But there are two principal reasons for that hostility. One has been generated by NATO itself in the form of its expansion in the 1990s up to the borders of Russia. The veteran American diplomat and Soviet expert George Kennan said in 1997 that "expanding NATO would be the most fateful error of American policy in the entire post-Cold War era" and might be expected "to restore the atmosphere of the Cold War to East-West relations." It has not been so dramatic in its consequences but it has excited Russian concerns about their own security. The other reason is Russia's resentment of Western interference in one of the countries directly located on its border – Ukraine – where the elected government was toppled by a coup in 2014 after the US had spent $5 billion in support of the opposition forces in that country.

French President Macron has said that NATO is "brain dead". It is not entirely clear what he meant by this but it does seem to be an organisation that has been overtaken by events so that there is now a real question as to its utility.

WAR AND PEACE

The role of Australia in the Vietnam War is still the subject of some enduring myths which are the subject of several of these articles. In particular, the notion that Australia entered the war because of pressure from the US is rejected on the basis of clear evidence that the Menzies government was anxious to become involved and concerned – without reason as it turned out - that Washington might bring the conflict to an end by negotiation.

There are also myths about the outbreak of the Great War in 1914, including the thesis that somehow this conflict erupted without any of the participants really desiring that end, whereas there is considerable evidence that some of them were determined on this result and others did little to prevent it.

Terrorism has now become an ever-present threat in Western countries but I have given a personal account of one of the first of these attacks at the Olympic Games in Munich in 1972. Other pieces, however, look at terrorism in its more recent context and raise the question of the rather ambiguous response to these incidents in many Western nations.

WAR AND PEACE

THE AUSTRALIAN FINANCIAL REVIEW

Wednesday 9 October 2002

THE FACTS OF US INTERVENTION

In the recent public debate concerning the events of September 11, 2001 and the possibility of action against Iraq some contributors appear to hold massive misconceptions about the United States' recent history.

Many of these myths seem to be based on a view that the US is responsible for all of the world's problems or that, even if it is not, it has a duty to deal with those problems. On the other hand, as soon as the US does intervene, directly or indirectly, in the affairs of another country, it is roundly criticised.

Myth No. 1: The United States and its allies were responsible for atrocities as bad as those of the Germans and Japanese in Second World War. The most commonly quoted examples are those of the bombing of Dresden and the use of the atomic bomb on Hiroshima and Nagasaki. This view seems to assume some kind of moral equivalence between the two sides in this conflict. The fact is that the Germans and the Japanese attempted to – and did – annex almost all of Europe and Asia, while at the same time exterminating large proportions of these populations. No rational person would celebrate the deaths of civilians – or of soldiers for that matter – but the allies were conducting a war for their survival.

Myth No. 2: The Americans dragged Australia into the Vietnam War. Vietnam was an enormous mistake by the United States. But it did not need Australia's military assistance. It was the Menzies government that hounded the Americans in late 1964 and early 1965 to allow Australian troops to be involved in the escalation of the war. The Americans at least had as one of their objectives the survival of an independent South Vietnam. The Australian government was totally indifferent to the fate of South Vietnam or its people. Its only interest was in creating an insurance policy in Washington in case of trouble with Indonesia.

Myth No. 3: The United States failed to prevent the killing of 800,000 persons in Rwanda in 1994. This is certainly one of the strangest suggestions to come out of the recent debate. It was the United Nations, through its people on the ground, who had some advance warning of the mass killing by Hutus of Tutsis. Were the Americans supposed to provide the major part of any UN intervention? If so, does this mean that they should have moved into Rwanda but should not intervene in Iraq?

Myth No. 4: The Americans failed to intervene in Bosnia and failed to intervene soon enough in Kosovo. There was a debate in Washington in the early 1990s about whether to try to separate the warring parties in Bosnia but most European countries refused to support intervention. Bosnia was, however, partitioned in 1995 into Serb and Muslim enclaves after negotiations presided over by American officials. The question of Kosovo blew up in 1997. Again, the Europeans – except for Britain – were against intervention but eventually, in 1999, grudgingly combined with the Americans – through NATO – to use air power to halt ethnic cleansing by the Serbs.

Myth No. 5: The failure to reach a settlement in the Middle East is due to American support for Israel. Is there any evidence that the Palestinians want a settlement? In 2000 Arafat rejected an offer that – for the first time – met most of the Palestinians' key demands. It might be noted that this offer was made in a negotiation presided over by President Clinton who had persuaded the Israelis to make this proposal. But it was rejected out of hand. If the position of the Palestinians and many of their Arab allies is that Israel has no future, there seems little point in the Israelis negotiating at all. They can hardly be worse off, no matter what they do. Israel could not afford to take a different position, whatever the view of the United States might be.

Let's have a debate about Iraq but without some of these modern history fables that seem to have clouded the issues over recent months.

THE AUSTRALIAN

February 2006

MUNICH 1972: DEATH AT THE OLYMPICS

On the night of 4 September 1972, when Black September personnel were preparing to attack the Israeli quarters in Munich's Olympic village, I was sitting at a crowded table in one of the city's noisiest beer halls.

The table was an odd mixture. There was a small group of recent graduates from Melbourne University law school. We were on a long camping tour of Europe and had decided to take in the Games. The rest of the table was occupied by members of the chorus of Milan's La Scala opera company which was performing in Munich. Everyone joined in some singing, although it was no surprise that the chorus had much better voices.

When the beer hall closed, we set off for our camping spot about 20 kilometres outside the town. All the official camping grounds were full so we simply chose a wood near the site of the former Dachau concentration camp. Its proximity to Munich was a reminder that the existence of such places was hardly a secret in the German community of the 1930s.

Next morning we awoke late. The litre steins of strong beer had taken a heavy toll. We heard the news about the village and, along with a lot of the locals, drove to that part of town. The village was in a bowl and it was possible to look down on it from the surrounding heights. Although so close to the scene, we knew less about what was happening than if we had been watching television on the other side of the world. But it was only much later that anyone found out the full story of that day.

It is possible to enjoy Steven Spielberg's new film, *Munich*, as a thriller. But there are two important points that it does not make. The first is that it does not highlight the moral distinction between the killing of a group of athletes by members of a para-military organisation and the later killing of some Black September operatives by members of an Israeli security organisation. It is normal in a wartime situation to expect soldiers to kill each other but not – by most moral standards – to intentionally kill civilians.

Putting aside this question, however, the film does not deal with the most extraordinary aspects of these events – the conduct of the German authorities in Munich and the attitude of the International Olympic Committee. The Munich police would not allow the Israelis to send a team from Israel to make an assault on the building occupied by Black September. We know – because all the captured athletes were ultimately killed – that no result of such an attack could have been any worst than the final outcome.

The Germans never launched an assault of their own. At one point they made plans for an attack but called it off when it became clear that the preparations were being televised to the world at large and so to the Black September invaders of the village. This was because the area around the occupied building had not even been sealed off from the media.

Later in the day the Germans agreed to a bizarre scheme under which the hostages and their captors would go by helicopter to a local airport where a plane would be provided by the authorities. This was to be a trap. The plane was occupied by armed police officers who would engage the terrorists. Shortly before the arrival at the airport of the helicopters carrying the hostages the police on the plane decided that this was a dangerous mission and *voted* to call it off! Without consulting any of their superiors, they then left the plane standing empty.

When the terrorists and the hostages approached the plane, there were some uncoordinated shots fired by snipers. The snipers were not professional marksmen. They had no radio contact with each other. None of the rifles carried scopes or night-vision sighters. Some of the terrorists survived and killed all the remaining athletes.

Three of the terrorists remained alive but, instead of being tried and imprisoned, they were released by the German government shortly afterwards in response to the supposed hijacking of a Lufthansa plane by Black September. So quickly was this arrangement arrived at that there are real grounds for suspicion that the government knew in advance of the hijacking and allowed it to occur so as to have an excuse to release the survivors.

This astonishing record of German incompetence – or worse – is the real story of the Munich Games. It should be noted, however, that the conduct of the IOC was dreadful in its own way. It grudgingly suspended the Games for two days but then resumed them as if nothing had happened.

The whole episode was a reminder to the Israelis of something they already knew – that they could expect no sympathy in Germany and little in the international community generally. Spielberg's film is careful to make no moral judgments. That is his choice but its audiences need to be aware of the historical realities.

THE SYDNEY MORNING HERALD

May 31-June 1, 2008

THE LASTING QUESTION: DID TERRORISM WIN?

Great Hatred, Little Room: Making Peace in Northern Ireland by Jonathan Powell

This is a diplomat's book, with all the strengths and weaknesses of that profession. Jonathan Powell, who had been up till then a member of the British foreign service, joined Tony Blair as chief of staff when Blair was Leader of the Opposition. After the general election of May 1997, they moved together into No. 10 Downing Street. This book is Powell's record of the negotiations during the next ten years, conducted largely by Blair and himself on the British side, over the future of Northern Ireland.

The background to the negotiations, however, was that the IRA had by this time broken the will of the British government. The IRA had always insisted that it was fighting a war and there was plenty of evidence of this. In 1979 they killed a Cabinet minister at Westminster; in 1984 they narrowly missed killing Margaret Thatcher in Brighton with a bomb that destroyed much of her hotel; and in 1991 they launched a rocket attack on No. ten Downing Street. But, if captured, they insisted on all the protections of the criminal justice system as if they were house burglars.

The British governments of the 1980s and 1990s were not prepared to make war on these terrorists and so ultimately were obliged to surrender to them. This is really acknowledged by Powell when he says of Blair and himself that "neither of us had any historical baggage on Northern Ireland ... We were of a younger generation and the war against Irish terrorism was not our war."

In addition to the British government, the negotiating parties were the Irish government, Sinn Fein – the so-called political wing of the IRA – and the various Unionist groups in Northern Ireland. Although they represented a majority of the population of Northern Ireland, the Unionist groups had two disadvantages. First, they had serious divisions between themselves, as the book notes in some detail. And second, they had no allies amongst the other parties. The British government was neutral and the Irish government almost invariably supported Sinn Fein.

Blair and Powell had an early success with the Good Friday agreement of 1998 that was approved by a referendum in both the Irish Republic and Northern Ireland and resulted in elections for a Northern Ireland Assembly. But, the following year the Assembly's Executive was suspended when the parties proved unable to work together. In the midst of all this came the Omagh bombing in August 1998 where members of the IRA killed 29 persons and wounded hundreds of others. Blair had always said that he would stop the negotiations if the IRA continued its campaign of terror but, when incidents like Omagh occurred, he pressed on anyway.

Because the book records the hundreds of meetings that took place over this decade, often in painstaking detail, it is a very valuable historical record. There is, however, in diplomatic tradition, a rather bloodless quality to Powell's account. There is a wide cast of unusual characters – including David Trimble, Gerry Adams, Ian Paisley, Tony Blair himself – but Powell misses the chance to draw graphic portraits of them. There is also a sense that there was nothing else except Northern Ireland going on over this period, whereas Blair was also occupied with Iraq, the Middle East and numerous domestic crises.

One external event, however, did have a significant impact on the negotiations. This was the destruction of the twin towers on 9/11.

Up to this time the IRA had always received a great deal of moral and financial support from some American groups. To some extent, although not entirely, the attitude of these groups towards terrorists was changed by an attack on their own country.

The book ends in May 2007 with the resumption of the Northern Island Assembly and an Executive led by Ian Paisley as First Minister and Martin McGuinness as his deputy. This is presented by Powell as something of a triumph, although the two sides in Northern Ireland remain in fundamental disagreement as to whether it should remain part of the United Kingdom.

Peter Mandelson, who was the Minister responsible for Northern Ireland in the British government for some of the period covered by the book, has said of Powell:

> Adams and McGuinness knew exactly who they were dealing with in Jonathan. They were playing with a public school boy who seemed to love being played with – and who too often acted as if he enjoyed being beguiled by their charm.

This is a harsh view and it may be that Blair and Powell did make a lasting change to the conflict in Northern Ireland. But it is hard to put this book down without an uneasy feeling that terrorism has – not for the first time – paid off.

THE AUSTRALIAN

Thursday, May 10, 2012

IF ONLY WE HAD KNOWN THE COST

What would have happened if Britain had not entered World War I in August 1914?

Over recent years there has been something of a revival of interest in the Great War, reflected in this country by the efforts to identify the final resting place of those Australians who died in France but have never been found. But one question that is seldom asked is whether the Great War could have been avoided – at least by Britain and the Empire.

It is true, of course, that the Germans were chiefly responsible for instigating the conflict by encouraging the Austrians to declare war on Serbia, although the stupidity of the Tsar and his advisors in ordering the mobilisation of the Russian army helped to ensure that there would be a clash of arms on the continent of Europe. And it is also true that the Germans invaded Belgium as the shortest route to Paris in accordance with the long-established Schlieffen Plan. It was this violation of Belgian territory that precipitated Britain's declaration of war on 4 August 1914. So there could be no doubt that at one level a response to Germany's aggression was justified.

But at another level no one could have foreseen the horrific consequences of the war. The best estimate of soldiers killed over the next four years is over nine million with another twenty-one million wounded, many of these having lost limbs or suffered permanent mental breakdowns. The losses of the Anzacs at Gallipoli was substantial but could not rival the slaughter on the Western front. On the first day of the Somme – 1 July 1916 – the British had 60,000 casualties with almost 20,000 of these dead. Even these figures take no account of the millions of civilian deaths through disease and starvation, including the victims of the influenza pandemic that followed immediately after the war and had its origins in disembarkation camps.

In the case of Australia the losses of military personal – almost sixty thousand out of a little over four hundred thousand troops – provided the highest proportion of casualties on the Empire side. This was a huge figure for a small – and still young – nation. It left a generation of widows and spinsters without men between the wars.

The political consequences of the war were equally devastating. German resentment at the terms imposed on them at Versailles may have been unjustified but it was a potent factor in Hitler's rise to power in the late 1920s and his final seizure of the machinery of government in 1933. It seems unlikely that the Second War would have occurred in the same way, if at all, in the absence of the First.

The same might be said about the Russian revolution which was largely a product of disillusionment amongst the soldiers of the Tsar's huge army. It might be argued – no doubt correctly – that some dramatic change was inevitable in Russia as the autocratic and utterly incompetent regime of Nicholas II collided with the realities of the 20th century. But an initial transition to a constitutional monarchy may have been possible without the colossal bloodshed of the civil war that followed the revolution and the taking of power by the Bolsheviks. And this may have averted the Stalin period of the 1920s and 1930s when millions lost their lives in purges and famines or were sent to labour camps in the Gulag, itself a sentence of death for all but a few hardy survivors.

What would have happened in Britain had not joined in the conflict in August 1914, taking the Empire with her? There seems little doubt that France would have been defeated and lost some territory. Probably there would have been a negotiated piece between

Germany and Russia as the Germans' real interest was to hold sway in Europe. The effect of the domination of continental Europe by Germany would have been a high price to pay for Britain and the rest of the world. But would this have been so different from the current position where almost all the nations of Europe – and some of the Balkans – are part of a political and economic union of which Germany is far and away the strongest and most influential member?

All this has, of course, the benefit of hindsight and the British Cabinet had to make its decision on the spot on 4 August 1914. On that day it had to decide whether to issue an ultimatum to Germany not to invade Belgium, knowing that the ultimatum would be rejected and that war would follow. Three junior ministers did resign when the ultimatum was issued but the rest stayed. Would they, however, have made the same decision if they had known what was to follow?

THE SYDNEY MORNING HERALD

June 9-10, 2012

AN INFAMOUS MISCARRIAGE OF JUSTICE HAD A LASTING IMPACT

The Dreyfus Affair by Piers Paul Read

"Better Hitler than Blum" was a common wish – later to be granted – in some conservative circles in France in the late 1930s. Leon Blum was a Jew and a socialist who had twice been Prime Minister over the period 1936-1938. This was a sentiment that captured almost half a century later some of the deep divisions reflected in the Dreyfus affair.

Piers Paul Read is the author of sixteen novels and several works of non-fiction. He has brought his considerable writing skills to be bear on one of the most extraordinary sagas in modern French history.

The facts of the affair were deceptively simple. In 1894 Captain Alfred Dreyfus was falsely accused of passing military secrets to the Germans after the contents of a wastepaper basket at the German Embassy in Paris – passed on by an employee in the pay of the French – disclosed an unsigned letter from an officer in the French Army. After a court martial where evidence was suppressed, Dreyfus was subjected to a public degradation and then sent to Devil's Island off the coast of Guiana. The book's descriptions of his imprisonment are particularly graphic. Confined alone in a small hut on the site of a former leper colony, Dreyfus endured stifling heat and savage insects before being put in chains every night.

When Dreyfus' family organised some press coverage of his

plight, the official cover-up escalated dramatically. New evidence was concocted and the head of army intelligence, who refused to cooperate, was posted to Tunisia and then later dismissed without his pension. Emile Zola's famous press denunciation in 1898 resulted in his prosecution for libel and sentence to a year's imprisonment, which he avoided by fleeing to England. Even when Dreyfus was brought back to France for a second court martial in 1899 the original verdict was confirmed. Dreyfus was persuaded to accept a presidential pardon but there was also an amnesty for everyone else involved. Finally, in 1906 he was declared innocent by a civil court, reinstated in the army – only briefly because his health had been broken – and decorated.

It was, of course, hardly surprising that initially senior figures in the government and the army resisted the loss of face that would result from the overturning of the original verdict. But, as the book demonstrates, the affair came to divide French society in a much deeper fashion. The fate of Dreyfus himself became something of a sideshow. For the defenders of the army, it no longer mattered whether Dreyfus was guilty or not. As one of the generals said to the uncooperative head of army intelligence: "What does it matter to you if that Jew stays on Devil's Island?" On the other side, Dreyfus was a difficult hero – wealthy, shy, stiff, self-righteous and unfaithful to his devoted wife.

Read traces these events back to the French Revolution when supporters of the monarchy and the church were vanquished – but far from extinguished – by republicans and secularists. The fortunes of these two broad groups waxed and waned over the next century but remained the essential fault line in French politics. One side feared the influence of Jews and Freemasons while the other was always wary of a Jesuit conspiracy. By the 1890s this potent cocktail of phobias was made more volatile by anti-German sentiments in the wake of France's crushing defeat in the war of 1871 and the subsequent loss of its provinces of Alsace and Lorraine. Officers in the army reflected these two strains in society, some being a product of Jesuit academies and others from secular institutions.

Read himself brings a Catholic perspective to this period of French history. He acknowledges, however, that most Catholics were anti-Dreyfusards and does not shrink from their worst excesses, although he also details the dissolution of the religious orders by legislation in 1901.

Showing that passions still ran high, Dreyfus was shot and wounded in 1908 at the public function when Zola's ashes were transferred to the Panthéon. His attacker was charged with attempted murder but acquitted to shouts from the court's gallery that Dreyfus was always guilty. Dreyfus returned to the colours in 1914 and saw action in the Great War. In a last act to this great drama, one of his granddaughters joined the Resistance in early 1940s and died in Auschwitz. The Vichy regime that took office under the German occupation were in many ways the last heirs of the anti-Dreyfusards but the divisions highlighted by the affair can still be glimpsed from time to time in the France of 2012.

THE AUSTRALIAN

Tuesday, May 13, 2014

WHY WE PUSHED U.S. INTO AN UNWINNABLE WAR

Vietnam suited Australia's agenda

In his new book, *Dangerous Allies*, Malcolm Fraser suggests that Australia should repudiate the ANZUS Treaty and reject its longstanding alliance with the US.

He cites the Vietnam War as the classic case where the Australian government was trying to assist American political objectives rather than having in mind Australian strategic interests.

But Fraser has missed the point of Australia's involvement in the Vietnam War. Australia's commitment of ground troops to Vietnam was announced on April 29, 1965, by prime minister Robert Menzies but the key period for this decision was November 1964 to February 1965.

With the election of Lyndon Johnson in early November, policymakers in Washington were considering US options in Vietnam.

There were divisions within the administration. Defence secretary Robert McNamara remained optimistic, although undersecretary of state George Ball sent McNamara a memorandum saying "we are engaged in a fruitless struggle we are bound to lose" and Maxwell Taylor, US ambassador in Saigon, wrote that "the counter insurgency program countrywide is bogged down and will require heroic treatment to ensure revival". It is important to note that at this time the Americans did not have ground forces in Vietnam, only military advisers.

On December 14, 1964, the Australian government received a formal request from the Americans for additional advisers and some military equipment. But it responded on December 18 to say that the advisers and equipment could not be supplied but a commitment of Australian ground troops was possible.

This was an utterly cynical exercise by the Australian government, largely driven by Menzies and foreign minister Paul Hasluck. There was never any concern for South Vietnam itself but simply a desire to lock the Americans into a conflict in Southeast Asia and to have them indebted to Australia through its supply of a token troop force.

This objective in turn was fuelled by a deep-seated concern in Canberra about the threat the Australian government considered Indonesia posed to this country. So far from putting American interests before those of Australia, Menzies and Hasluck were prepared to push the US into an unwinnable war to suit what they saw as Australian strategic objectives.

This is why there was increasing concern in Canberra about the debate inside the Washington administration on the merits of deeper involvement in Vietnam.

In a cable sent by Keith Waller, Australian ambassador in Washington, to Hasluck on December 22, 1964, Waller complained about "the somewhat irresolute American attitude which gives cause for increasing uneasiness". In early January 1965 Hasluck told the acting head of his department that he was "gravely concerned" at the hesitancy of the Americans.

Later in January Hasluck asked Waller to use arguments that would "reinforce the persuasions of any like-minded elements within the United States administration", and added: "I fear above all the likelihood of slipping into negotiation by default".

This last comment by Hasluck is a particularly telling one. It indicates the concern in Canberra that the conflict in Vietnam might be brought to a halt by international negotiations.

The prospect of negotiations had been raised by French president

Charles de Gaulle and also by the British government. But that was not what the Australian government wanted.

It hoped not only for the continuation of the conflict but for its escalation with considerably increased American involvement. Given the later disastrous history of the war, this position was not in America's long-term interest. But Canberra had its own agenda and was quite indifferent to the interests of the US and South Vietnam.

In February the Australian government finally got its wish when heavy bombing of North Vietnam by US aircraft began and the landing of 3500 marines in South Vietnam was approved. This US ground force would swell to 525,000 by 1967.

It took until mid-April 1965 for Canberra to obtain a formal request for Australian ground troops from Washington but, as the documents from this period demonstrate, Canberra's response was not a case of Australian subservience to American interests but one of Australia's view of its own self-interest.

Fraser did not become a minister until 1966 but he was a MP when these decisions were made and he should have had a better understanding of the history of this period.

THE AUSTRALIAN

Wednesday, April 29, 2015

U.S. DIDN'T PRESSURE US INTO VIETNAM, WE WERE URGING THEM TO ESCALATE

Unlike the Anzacs, our military adventure in Indochina was less than glorius

This is a week for anniversaries. Not only the centenary of the ANZAC landings at Gallipoli but also 50 years since the announcement of Australia's entry into the Vietnam War. On 29 April 1965 Prime Minister Sir Robert Menzies announced to the federal parliament that Australia would commit almost 1,000 combat troops to the conflict in Vietnam. By October 1967 the total number of Australian military personnel in Vietnam had reached over 8,000.

There are several long-standing myths about Australia's participation in the Vietnam War. One is that the Whitlam government withdrew their remaining Australian troops after its election in December 1972. In fact, all the troops had been withdrawn by the end of 1971 during the period of the McMahon government.

Another myth is that the war was deeply unpopular in the Australian community. The feeling in the electorate was demonstrated in the 1966 general election when the Liberal government, under Prime Minister Harold Holt, won in a landslide after Labor had come out against the decision to commit troops. It is true that the community was more evenly divided on the question of conscription but it was not until later in the 1960s, when it was clear that the war was going badly for the US and its allies, that public opinion in Australia became disenchanted with continued participation in the conflict.

Perhaps the most persistent myth, however, is that the Australian government was pressured by the Americans to make a commitment of ground troops. As it happens, there was a debate in Washington in late 1964 and early 1965, following Lyndon Johnson's victory in the November presidential election, as to whether the US would significantly increase its role in Vietnam. The Australian government, particularly Menzies and foreign Minister, Paul Hasluck, pushed the Washington administration to escalate its war effort and to ask for the presence of Australian troops. The diplomatic cables between the government in Canberra and the Australian Embassy in Washington over this period indicate a concern on the Australian side that the US might enter into negotiations with North Vietnam and that the war might come to an end.

The Australian government's objectives were certainly fulfilled. The first American combat troops landed in Vietnam in March 1965. There were 1,500 of them. Two months later there were 50,000 and by the end of 1965 there were 200,000. By the middle of 1967 there were 525,000. The last Americans were evacuated from Saigon on 30 April 1975, the day on which North Vietnamese troops entered the city. More than two million persons had been killed in the course of the war and twice than number wounded. Twice as many again had been made refugees.

Some commentators in the US and Australia now say that the decision to intervene in Vietnam was right but that the war was fought in the wrong way. They suggest that it is only in hindsight that it looks obvious that the drastic military means necessary to win the war could not be undertaken once the political will of the American administration had been eroded by public loss of confidence in victory. But there were members of the Johnson administration who had put forcefully, if unsuccessfully, the view that the war was unwinnable in late 1964 and early 1965 in Washington. In May 1961 French president Charles de Gaulle said to US president John Kennedy whom he liked despite their somewhat different personalities, that intervention in Vietnam would be an "entanglement without end". The French, of course, had been defeated by the North Vietnamese forces in 1954 and forced to withdraw from the region. De Gaulle added to Kennedy his prediction that "you will, step by step, become sucked into a bottomless military and political quagmire despite the losses and expenditure that you may squander".

Menzies was one of the most talented persons to become an Australian Prime Minister but Vietnam is a significant stain on his record period of leadership. This was a particularly cynical exercise on the Australian side because it was an attempt to lock the Americans into the south-east Asian region without ultimately caring what the consequences of the war were for the US. Vietnam has cast a long shadow for the US. It still today affects its attitude to foreign interventions and it remains the source of some hostility and much suspicion amongst the people of European nations. Unlike the ANZAC experience, Vietnam was one of the least glorious exercises in Australian military and political history.

SPECTATOR AUSTRALIA

1 July 2017

TERRORISM NOTES

A strange game

The organisers of terrorist attacks in various European cities over recent times seem to seriously misunderstand the impact of these incidents on the nations of the West.

The truth is that most of the political class and many members of the community in these countries are not dismayed by these attacks but regard them, somewhat cynically, as an unavoidable aspect of this period of history. If the terrorists expect to sap the morale of Western countries, they are mistaken, not because of a heroic spirit of resistance in those nations but because of a widespread indifference to these events. This explains why recent events in London, Paris, Berlin, Nice and Manchester have disappeared from press coverage within a few days of their happening and then appear to be largely forgotten. The initial reaction is one of well-meaning but pious platitudes by political leaders and collections of flowers and candles from locals or tourists visiting the site of the killings but again these quickly come to an end.

In the case of the Bali bombings of 2002, where 88 Australians were killed, it was only a matter of weeks before holiday-makers from Australia returned to Kuta Beach. This is not to be critical of those visiting the resort so soon from this and other countries but it does indicate the way in which terrorist attacks fade rapidly from collective memory.

This is not to say that most members of the community share the delusion of some commentators that there is no problem about terrorism because there is a greater likelihood of, for example, being killed in a traffic accident. Nor are they as naïve as the Dean of Westminster, Dr John Hall, presiding over a national church service in the wake of the London attack in March, who said: "What could possibly motivate a man to hire a car and take it from Birmingham to Brighton to London and then drive it fast at people he had never met, couldn't possibly know, against whom he had no personal grudge, no reason to hate them, and then run at the gates of the Palace of Westminster to cause another death? It seems likely we shall never know." Most members of the community, of course, do know but they are not interested in the political dimension of the problem, viewing the victims in the same detached way that they would regard those killed in a plane crash or a shark attack who are not amongst their own family and friends.

This widespread indifference to terrorist attacks is reflected in the follow-up investigation and reporting – or lack of these, although Manchester was initially something of an exception. Why is it that in most of these cases nothing is ever heard afterwards about the background of those who were identified as gunman, bombers or drivers? How did they come to be where they were? Where did they obtain their weapons or vehicles? What were their sources of funds? Who else was involved in these activities?

This last question appears to be one that the law enforcement authorities in most countries are anxious to avoid. The driving attacks in London, Berlin and Nice were quickly described as "lone wolf" actions in which no one else was involved. This description could, however, hardly be applied to the co-ordinated attacks in several parts of Paris and the use of a sophisticated explosive device in Manchester. As it happens, the driving attack in Nice, where 86 persons were killed, did not seem to be a "lone wolf" exercise as six other persons were charged by the French authorities as accomplices in relation to a terrorist enterprise. But almost a year later there are still no reports as to what has happened to those charges or whether these six individuals were in fact involved, and if so how, in the attack.

One of the most puzzling aspects of these recent events has been the initial reluctance of the authorities to even name the person or persons who have carried out the attack when they have been identified. This concern presumably arises from the fact that, almost without exception, all of the attacks over a period of many years have been carried out by persons of similar profile and background. Which raises the question why security officers at airports around the world can be seen body-searching 70 year old women on literary tours. Why are law enforcement agencies so reluctant to admit where the threat comes from? It hardly seems a good starting point for dealing with that threat.

On this question, the authorities in Manchester complained bitterly that the name of the suicide bomber and some images of what was left of the bomb were published in the American media, supposedly from information provided by US intelligence agencies from their British counterparts. Putting aside the issue of the relationship between intelligence bodies in different countries, the real question is why this information had not been released by the British authorities. It would seem a matter of significant public interest and it is hard to see how it could hinder future investigations when the terrorists must assume that law enforcement bodies have examined scene of the attack.

It is difficult to say how this deadly cycle might be broken in the immediate future. The terrorists seem unaware that their actions are having no significant impact on Western society, except perhaps for the non-targeted and inefficient security procedures that now occur at all international and domestic airports. It is hardly reassuring that law enforcement bodies in all these countries will not publicly – possibly even privately – identify the small groups in their communities who are the obvious source of almost all terrorist activities. It is a strange conflict where one side cannot see the futility of its actions and the other side cannot admit who the enemy really is.

THE SYDNEY MORNING HERALD

November 3-4, 2018

OUR MAN ON THE BLOODY FRONT LINE

The Western Front Diaries of Charles Bean, Ed. Peter Burness

There is no shortage of writing by and about Charles Bean, Australia's sole official war correspondent for most of the years of the Great War. Following the war he published his Gallipoli diaries and oversaw the Australian official history of the conflict, writing six of the twelve volumes himself. There have also been several biographies of Bean. Now Peter Burness has assembled a vast collection of extracts from Bean's diaries during his time on the Western Front between April 1916 and November 1918.

Bean was born in Bathurst in 1879 but educated in England, reading classics and law at Oxford. He returned to Australia and joined the *Sydney Morning Herald* in 1908. At the outbreak of the war in August 1914 he was appointed Australia's only official war correspondent and filed many reports from Gallipoli after the ANZAC landings there in April 1915 before moving to the Western Front early in 1916.

Despite its cover price, this book is a remarkable bargain. In addition to being printed on high quality paper, it contains not only the diary entries but also hundreds of photos, maps, drawings, explanatory notes and miniature biographies of many of the characters referred to in the diary extracts.

During the war years Bean moved in high circles, having almost open access to visiting Australian politicians, including the Prime Minister, Billy Hughes and to the highest ranking military personnel. His diaries make it clear that, despite being surrounded by constant slaughter, he believed in the war, at least in the sense that the soldiers could only go home when the war had been won. This no doubt made it easier for him to accept the rigorous censorship that was applied by the military authorities to all information about the war, although even Bean complained about this on occasions.

Not only were accounts of the fighting heavily sanitised but no photos were allowed that might show the true nature of the conflict. Bean's photo of stretcher bearers carrying wounded across no-man's land was prohibited because it showed them carrying a white flag and this was considered as undermining the war effort. References to the mud in which so much of the fighting took place were also unacceptable because this might affect civilian morale at home. It is interesting to speculate whether support for the war could have been maintained if its full horrors had been publicised. Certainly public opinion about the Vietnam War was significantly affected by television coverage of the conflict.

Not surprisingly perhaps, given Bean's general acceptance of the war, there is no real discussion in the diaries of whether there was any alternative to the British strategy of attrition, orchestrated by its senior commander, General Haig, and the cause, for example, of 20,000 British dead on the first day of the Somme, 1 July 1916. One of the few commanders who attempted some refinement of this strategy was the Australian general, John Monash, generally accepted as one of the best military minds on the allied side. Bean, however, was consistently hostile to Monash, arguing that "we do not want Australia represented by men mainly because of their ability, natural and inborn in Jews, to push themselves." So too was Keith Murdoch, an Australian journalist and close friend of Bean's who was then based in London but became a press baron in his later career in Australia. Bean was also scathing in his view of the British army: "Generals without brains and an army without physique – and there you have it."

Sometimes the diaries capture graphically the awful prospect confronting the new arrival at the front:

> This new force of ours is just realising … that there is only one way out of this war for an infantryman – and that is on his back; either sick, wounded, or dead … they will be put out to fight and fight and fight again – until if not in this battle then in the next each man gets his bullet. There is no way out.

Again, however, consistently with his view of the war, Bean was in favour of conscription in Australia and disappointed when it was rejected at two plebiscites in October 1916 and December 1917, particularly when even the soldiers overseas voted "no" on the second occasion.

This book makes accessible an important piece of Australian history and both the editor and the publisher deserve congratulations for it.

AUSTRALIAN BOOK REVIEW

20 May 2019

MYTHS OF WAR

Australia's Vietnam: Myth vs History by Mark Dapin

Almost all historical events are attended by myths, some of them remarkably persistent, but Australia's involvement in the Vietnam war has perhaps more than its fair share. Mark Dapin has set out to dispel what he sees as six of these myths which he first encountered working on his book *The Nashos' War* published in 2014.

The first myth is that all the national servicemen who went to Vietnam volunteered for this assignment. This proposition is repeated in various Australian texts about the war but Dapin demonstrates that it is not true. It was true that in the Great War and almost entirely in the Second World War all the Australians who served overseas were volunteers and the same applied to those who were part of the national service scheme of the 1950s and posted outside Australia. But the whole point of the conscription ballot introduced in late 1964 by the Menzies government was to boost the numbers of the army with men who could be sent to fight overseas. This was the government's explicit policy and it would have been completely undermined if national servicemen had been allowed to refuse to go to Vietnam when their unit was posted there.

Dapin's second myth is that the ballot under which some birth dates were drawn was in some way fixed to obtain, for example, persons with particular occupations. I doubt that this was ever generally believed but the book is interesting about the kinds of groups who became national servicemen. One reason that they do not seem to have been an entire cross-section of the community is that the scheme only lasted for eight years and deferments for full-time study meant that, at least in the early years, there would have been very few university graduates, although it must be remembered that, in comparison with today, only a very small number of persons attended university in Australia.

The third myth is that there were no parades for returning soldiers as there had been in earlier wars. As it happens, the book notes that, for logistic reasons, there were few home-coming parades in 1918 and 1945. In contrast, there were welcoming crowds of several hundred thousand in Sydney for troops returning from Vietnam in every year between 1966 and 1969. This myth seems to have arisen from a feeling on the part of some of the troops that their role in Vietnam was not properly recognised on their return. This may be closer to the truth, given the fact that after the fall of Saigon in 1975 it was obvious that the allied forces had lost the war. Arguably, however, because this was the first conflict in which Australia had been involved that did not have the support of the great bulk of the community, it was clear from the outset that this would be different from earlier wars and that those returning would never be viewed as heroes like their predecessors.

Somewhat allied to the notion of no homecoming parades, are the fourth and fifth myths – that returning troops were met by protests when they arrived at airports in Australia and that they were the subject of abuse, and in some cases, physical attack, once back in Australia. Dapin examines all the accounts of these allegations and concludes, correctly in my view, that, except for one isolated incident, there was no evidence for any of them. In relation to airport protests, for example, he notes the absence in ASIO records of any reference to them, despite this being a time when ASIO operatives attended and recorded almost all protests against the war. On the question of public abuse of returned soldiers, it is certainly my recollection from the time that this did not occur and one reason why it didn't was that those groups who were opposed to the war did not see Australia's role in Vietnam as the responsibility of army personnel but of the national government that had sent them there.

The final myth is that of war crimes committed by Australians in Vietnam. Despite some anecdotal accounts, Dapin was unable to find any hard evidence for this, although doubtless there were many untargeted civilians who suffered or perished because of their proximity to military engagements by all parties.

It is not put forward as one of Dapin's myths but there does seem to be an assumption in some later accounts of the Vietnam period that the war was always unpopular in the Australian community. It is true that the conflict did not have the whole-hearted support of earlier wars but the Liberals, under the leadership of Harold Holt following Menzies' retirement, won what was then the largest election victory in Australian political history in 1966. The war was one of the foremost issues in the poll because of Labor's opposition to the troop commitment that had been made in 1965. As the book points out, a Gallup poll in December 1968 still showed 49 per cent of respondents with the opinion that Australia should stay in Vietnam and 37 per cent that its troops should be withdrawn. This was at a time when it might be thought that it had become obvious that the war could not be won and the debate in the United States on its continuation had become widespread. These years were not the Australian electorate's finest hour. The majority of the community was prepared to allow a small group, chosen by lot, to risk their lives in a conflict that had no impact on anyone else in that community. It was selfish and irresponsible behaviour that still leaves a bad taste fifty years later.

It might be assumed from some other accounts of this period that universities at least were oases of radicalism and so did not reflect the rest of the community. In fact only a very small minority of university students had any real interest in politics and only some of those were actively opposed to the war. In something of a contrast to many of their counterparts in the US, Australian universities at the time did largely reflect the views of society as a whole.

One early myth that may have been, partially at least, dispelled by later histories is that the Australian government was pressured by Washington to make its first significant commitment of ground troops in April 1965. The exchanges between Canberra and Washington indicate, however, that the Australians, particularly Foreign Minister, Paul Hasluck, effectively solicited the invitation from the Americans to become involved in the conflict at a serious level. Moreover, in early 1965 they urged Washington to step up the war at a time when there was still some debate in the US administration as to what was the best course to take in Vietnam.

This book is a valuable contribution to the history of Australia's involvement in the Vietnam War. It will, however, bring little comfort to the Australian soldiers who fought in this misguided and misjudged conflict.

THE AUSTRALIAN

11 November 2019

EUROPE HARDLY 'STUMBLED' INTO GREAT WAR

The thought of Germany holding France was too much for other regional powers

November 11, 1918 – when the guns stopped firing in the Great War – is still widely marked as Remembrance Day but historians have always been more interested in how and why the war commenced in July 1914.

There have been thousands of books published on this question but one of the most fashionable schools of thoughts in recent times has put forward the notion that the major powers of Europe stumbled into the conflict by accident, often accompanied by the suggestion that this could still happen today in the case of China, Russia and the US.

But the European powers did not stumble blindly into war in July 1914. It is true that the assassination of Austrian Archduke Franz Ferdinand in Sarajevo on 28 June 1914 by Serbian nationalists set the match to Europe's simmering cauldron of hatreds but a number of nations were only waiting for the right opportunity to unleash their military machines.

First amongst these opportunists was the Austro-Hungarian empire whose army chiefs had been looking for years for an excuse to invade and subdue Serbia. This is why the Austrian ultimatum to the Serbs following Franz Ferdinand's killing was couched in terms that could only be rejected. The Austrians did not want a resolution of the dispute. They wanted war and they did not care if this led to a wider conflict, provided that they had the support of Germany if that occurred.

And, they did have the support of Germany. Despite having comprehensively defeated France in the Franco-Prussian war of 1870, the German general staff were concerned that the balance of power in Europe was shifting in favour of the French and their ally, the Russians. The German solution to this problem was to attack and conquer France while the Austrians held off the Russians in the east and to do so before any further time passed.

As for the French, many of their decision-makers also looked forward to war with Germany. Notwithstanding the events of 1870, they saw the French army as indestructible and a successful conflict as a way of wresting back from the Germans the two provinces of Alsace and Lorraine that had been lost in the last war.

Serbia was smaller than these powers but just as bellicose. The assassins of Franz Ferdinand had been supported at a high level in the Serbian government and they had no qualms about war with Austria, provided, however, that they had the support of Russia in any conflict.

The two major powers that were not hell bent on war were Russia and England. But when Austria declared war on Serbia on 28 July 1914 the Russians allowed themselves to be dragged into the approaching maelstrom. Britain's position was more complicated because it had no forces on the continent of Europe and some members of its Liberal government were strongly opposed to entering the conflict. When Britain joined with France and Russia, it did so ostensibly on the ground that Belgium's sovereignty had been violated when it was invaded by the Germans. Its real reason, however, was to preserve the balance of power in Europe that would have been fundamentally changed by the defeat of France by Germany, a result that would almost certainly have occurred in the absence of British participation. Even then, it required the entry of the US into the war in 1917 to ensure the defeat of the Germans.

Did any of the politicians, generals and diplomats who were involved in these events foresee a conflict that would last for more than four years and cost the lives of ten million soldiers and eight million civilians? Some presumably did. As the editorial of the *Economist* said on 8 August 1914: "It is perhaps the greatest tragedy of human history … it may perhaps be the last time the working classes of the Continent will allow themselves to be marched to destruction at the dictates of diplomacy and by the order of their warlords." Not a bad call in the first week of the war.

The aftermath of the Great War was just as terrible. Without the war, it is possible that the Russian Revolution would never have happened in the way that it did and so been followed by the enormous loss of life in the civil war and then Stalin's purges and famines. It is also arguable that Hitler would not have been able to overrun Europe in 1940 if Russia had not been removed as a European power by the Revolution.

There is no doubt that the Great War has cast a long shadow over modern history, although few might have predicted that a century later Europe would be largely dominated by a partnership between France and Germany.

BREXIT AND THE EUROPEAN SUPER STATE

The 2016 British referendum on Brexit was essentially a contest between the concepts of national sovereignty and the supra-national European Union. After the vote for Brexit, however, the EU and most bodies of power and influence in Britain itself set out to frustrate this result. Ultimately they were unsuccessful but this was one of the rare occasions in modern history where the popular will prevailed over the forces that normally determine significant political decisions.

One important incidental question in all of this is the future of Scotland and Northern Ireland, both of which voted against Brexit. The governing Scottish National Party remains determined on a second referendum on the question of Scotland leaving the United Kingdom and the changing demography of Northern Ireland means that at some time in the immediate future the issue of its re-uniting with the Irish Republic will have to be considered.

BREXIT AND THE EUROPEAN SUPER STATE

THE AUSTRALIAN

Monday, June 5, 2017

UNGRATEFUL EUROPEANS OUT TO PUNISH UK

Brexit negotiations won't be easy but self-government is a worthwhile reward

In the unlikely event, Theresa May's Conservatives win a substantial victory in the British election on 8 June, it will certainly strengthen her hand in the Brexit negotiations with the European Community. But the negotiations, while always going to be difficult, are likely to also be very acrimonious.

This is because the Eurocrats in Brussels are extremely angry over Britain's withdrawal from the European Union. These politicians and officials see themselves as belonging to no particular country but administering a super state that takes no account of traditional borders or national identities. The three most important components of this empire were Germany, France and Britain. And now one of them has left.

The determination in Brussels to avoid the departure of any EU member country has been demonstrated by the effective take-over of Greece's huge debts. Everyone knows that these loans will never be repaid but the pretence is maintained that austerity measures introduced by the Greek government will ultimately deal with the problem. In the same vein, there has been public silence in Brussels about the failure of the current regimes in Hungary and Poland to accept EU solutions to some of their internal political disputes, although behind the scenes in Brussels there is considerable distaste for these two administrations.

The bitterness of the group towards the British was reflected in the comment of Jean Claude Junker, EU President and himself a native of the tiny principality of Luxembourg, that Brexit was "a failure and a tragedy" and his sneering remark that "the negotiations are now in the hands of our capable divorce lawyers." Junker's contempt for the views of the electorates in European countries was captured in his statement about a French referendum on the EU constitution: "If it is a Yes, we will say 'on we go', and if it is a No we will say 'we continue'". In 2016 he said publicly that "borders are the worst invention ever made by politicians."

This attitude of the Brussels political class has led them to impose an immigration policy on EU members that has resulted in a constant threat of terrorist acts and a series of actual attacks in various European cities, including London, Paris, Berlin, Nice and Manchester, in recent times. When the citizens of Paris see heavily-armed troops patrolling the Champs Elysées they might wonder at the price they have paid for the willingness of their own leaders to accept the dictates of the one-world technocrats in Brussels.

There is something extraordinary about Britain receiving moral lectures from the French and Germans when it is little more than 70 years – a span of less than one life time – since the Germans murdered a significant portion of the European population and France only survived as a nation because it was saved by the British and the Americans.

As if Britain did not face enough hostility from the EU, it also faces undermining from within the United Kingdom by Scotland and Northern Ireland, both of whom voted to remain in the EU. The Scottish Nationalists, having effectively used the issue of independence over the years to create a one-party state, now want to have a second plebiscite on leaving the UK. The notion of Scotland as a separate political and economical entity is simply fanciful. The British government should never have allowed the first plebiscite in 2014 and should certainly not countenance a second vote.

Similarly, Northern Ireland is hardly viable as a separate political and economic unit. It can either be part of the United Kingdom or part of the Irish Republic. It might be assumed that the non-Catholic half of its population, whatever their views on Brexit, would not relish joining the Republic. As it happens, there is little enthusiasm amongst the political leaders in the Republic for a takeover of Northern Ireland, given the fact that this would destabilise the existing balances of power between the political parties in Dublin. The only exception is, of course, Sinn Fein whose aim of a United Ireland led them to support decades of terrorism through their so-called military wing, the IRA.

It is fashionable to suggest that the Brexit vote was the product of uninformed prejudice by voters who were concerned about existing levels of immigration into Britain. It may be that this was an important factor in the minds of some of those who voted to leave the EU but immigration is one aspect of the real issue at the heart of the plebiscite – whether Britain was to govern itself or to be governed by foreign politicians and bureaucrats in Brussels. Under EU policies no member country can control the numbers of persons taking up residence within its borders.

Another aspect of the sovereignty question is the EU convention on human rights that overrides national laws and transfers power from elected parliamentarians to unelected judges. So British courts have been required to declare invalid legislation of the British parliament on the basis of a convention that was never initiated or drafted by the British parliament.

Reversing these decades of interference in its internal affairs by Brussels will not be an easy process for Britain but there is a lot to be said for self-government.

THE SPECTATOR AUSTRALIA

27 January 2018

BORDER WARS

The EU's contempt for national sovereignty has echoes of 1914

At the end of last year the European Union delivered an ultimatum to the Polish government. It gave the administration in Warsaw three months to change some of its policies or face the loss of voting rights in the EU and a cut-off of EU funds starting from 2021.

The measures of Poland's governing Law and Justice Party that have aroused particular distaste in Brussels are its efforts to institute greater government control over some aspects of the court system and the national broadcasting network. It is not necessary to endorse these policies, however, to think that they are matters for the elected government of the day and decisions that can be reversed if they prove sufficiently unpopular with the electorate to result in the rejection of the ruling party at the next election.

Similar sanctions have been threatened by Brussels against the government of Hungary with its Fidesz party led by Viktor Orbán. As in the case of Poland, Brussels disapproves of administration policies affecting the operations of the media. In the case of both countries there is also strong disapproval amongst EU bureaucrats of their resistance to EU positions on the volume of immigration from outside the Union. Again all these are matters for debate but debate, it might be thought, within Poland and Hungary.

That, however, is not a view held in Brussels. Jean Claude Junker, EU president and a native of the toy town principality of Luxembourg, said publicly last year that "borders are the worst invention ever made by politicians". His contempt for the opinions of electors in member countries was indicated by his statement some years ago about a French referendum on the EU constitution: "If it is a Yes, we will say 'on we go', and if it is a No, we will say 'we continue'." Martin Schulz, who was at one time president of the European Parliament and last year became leader of Germany's Social Democrats, said during the negotiations over Greece's financial plight that it was time for a "government of technocrats" to replace those who had been elected to office in Athens. No one would defend the maladministration of Greek governments over a long period of time but this kind of statement reflects the indifference of EU politicians to the role of the electorate in individual countries.

This question of national sovereignty was at the heart of the Brexit referendum in Britain. It is fashionable, of course, for the opponents of Brexit to say that those who voted to leave the EU were too ignorant to even know the meaning of the term and that their vote was the product of ill-informed prejudices. As the *Sydney Morning Herald* headlined its editorial of 23 June 2016: "A victory for hate should Brexit prevail". The editorial went on to say that "too many on the Leave side have appealed to the base instincts of susceptible people". It just may be, however, that a majority of the voters placed some value on the capacity of Britain to make decisions for itself, as it had done for centuries, rather than have them imposed by an external administrative body.

This was certainly the view of Clement Attlee, the British Labour leader, in 1950 when he rejected British participation in what was to be the first step on the way to the EU – the European Coal and Steel Community: "We have always been willing, and are now, to enter into … international arrangements, but the point of this plan was that it was something entirely different from the international arrangements. This was to set up a supra-national authority." And one, he added, that was "utterly undemocratic and responsible to nobody."

Despite the hostility to immigrants that was supposedly reflected in the Brexit vote, there is a large contingent of illegal immigrants camped at Calais and demanding entry to Britain. For some reason they seem to much prefer Britain to France, although one solution would be for EU stalwart, French President Emmanuel Macron, to persuade them to stay in France. But he says that they should be given entry by the British government and is using the Brexit negotiations to exert pressure on Britain to accept these groups. Given the terrorists attacks in recent times in London, Paris, Manchester and Nice, the citizens of both countries might wonder at the price that has been paid for the EU policy that no member country can control the inflow of persons across its borders.

What the aftermath of Brexit has demonstrated in Britain is the contempt for the electorate's vote on the part of the politically correct class who dominate almost all public and private institutions in Britain, as they do in Australia. This group spends much of its time moving across national boundaries for work and travel and places great faith in international organisations like the UN and so-called international law that would overrule domestic legislation. The idea of national sovereignty has, however, proved difficult to suppress in most parts of the world and even the EU is now experiencing resistance, in the form of Poland, Hungary and Britain, to its ideal of a world without borders.

Although for most of its members the EU is a supra-national body, it is in many ways a vehicle for the domination of Europe by Germany, as the senior partner, and France, as the junior partner. This is something of an irony, given that in 1914 Britain joined in the Great War essentially to prevent German domination of the European continent, although the decision was ostensibly taken because of treaty obligations concerning Belgium which had been invaded by the Germans at the outset of hostilities. The British decision was only taken after some internal debate and there must be a question in retrospect as to whether the enormous loss of British lives in the war only postponed a result that Germany has now achieved by political means.

THE AUSTRALIAN

Tuesday, January 22, 2019

BRUSSELS POUTS, SO MAY LEFT TO FIND BREXIT SOLUTION

The EU is mostly at fault for the fiasco overtaking the UK's economic future

The frantic negotiations taking place at Westminster between politicians on all sides in an effort to find a solution to the Brexit imbroglio have largely obscured the heavy responsibility the European Union bears for the crisis in Britain. Not that the EU administrators in Brussels would have any sympathy for their British counterparts. The present impasse underlines the fact that the European Union has long outgrown its original form as a trade agreement and become a supra-national state that has no interest in the views of the people in its member nations. As the former Greek finance minister, Yanis Varoufakis, has said of the EU, "it remains in the nature of the beast to treat the will of electorates as a nuisance that must be somehow negated."

This is why the EU establishment in Brussels never really accepted Britain's vote to leave the union and has always hoped for the reversal of that decision. For the French and the Germans in particular, the EU is not just about economics. It is essentially about a philosophy of power and anyone who rejects this quasi-religious view is not just misguided but guilty of a form of treachery.

It is hardly surprising, therefore, that the EU's negotiations with Britain have always been designed to frustrate the Brexit process, reflecting the view of European Commission president, Jean-Claude Juncker, that Brexit was "a failure and a tragedy." Juncker's contempt for the results of referendums was captured in his comment about an earlier French vote on the EU constitution: "If it is Yes, we will say 'on we go', and if it is a No, we will say 'we continue'". He is also on record as saying that "borders are the worst invention ever made by politicians."

The principal spoke that the EU negotiators inserted in the Brexit wheel has been the question of the border between the Irish Republic and the United Kingdom province of Northern Ireland. It is said that, although the Irish Republic will remain a member of the EU, there should be no customs procedures at the border with Northern Ireland. This issue is something of a mystery. What is the problem about having a customs system at a border between two countries? Of course those procedures are minimal between EU nations but the EU has borders with other non-member countries, such as Serbia and Turkey. This has been a cynical ploy by the EU negotiators, although the real puzzle is why Britain has accepted that this is a problem.

Consistently with its view that no member should be allowed to leave, the EU does not tolerate any differing views amongst its existing members. Hungary and Poland have been threatened with sanctions by Brussels because they refuse to subscribe to chancellor Merkel's notion of open borders on the basis that serious social and economic problems would inevitably follow from unrestricted immigration policies. As it happens, even Germany has been forced to retreat from its earlier position in the face of resistance to unregulated immigration from its own people.

The case of Greece illustrates the iron rule that Brussels tries – and in this instance succeeded – in imposing on member states. When it became clear that Greece was effectively bankrupt, the EU was determined that it should remain in the union but, in return for some financial assistance, forced the Greek government to agree to austerity measures that have had a dramatic impact on much of the population. The fact is that Greece is still bankrupt and will never be able to repay its outstanding loans. But for the EU the important thing is that the union remains intact. As president Macron has said what is crucial is "the integrity of the single market."

It was this notion of centralised control from Brussels that British foreign secretary, Jeremy Hunt, was referring to last year when he compared the EU to the former Soviet Union with its close supervision of its satellites in Eastern Europe. This was no doubt a provocative comment from the head of the diplomatic service and the parallels are hardly exact but there is a grain of truth in the comparison.

It is true that Mrs May's negotiating position has been made more difficult by divisions within her own party and the irresponsibility of the Opposition but the real problem in all of this has been the intransigence and bloody-mindedness of Brussels. If it had accepted the result of the British referendum and tried to facilitate rather than frustrate Britain's exit from the union, it is hard to imagine that the present crisis in Westminster would have occurred.

THE AUSTRALIAN

Friday, April 5, 2019

THE EU AND BREXIT'S ENEMIES WITHIN HAVE WRECKED THIS

Eurocrats traditionally ignore votes they don't like, as the UK is belatedly realising

It is necessary to remind ourselves occasionally that Britain had a referendum and voted to leave the European Union. In the light of subsequent events it is easy to lose sight of this seemingly obvious fact.

Why then has Brexit not happened? The chief reason is that the negotiations on the British side have been conducted with a series of mistakes that have led finally to the present imbroglio. To be fair to Mrs May, some of these mistakes are much clearer in retrospect than they may have seemed at the start of the negotiations. But one of the skills that politicians and civil servants are supposed to have is thinking ahead.

The first mistake was to assume that the negotiations on the British side could be effectively conducted by a group of ministers and bureaucrats, almost all of whom had supported the remain case and still believed that it was contrary to the nation's interests to leave the EU. This inevitably influenced, even if to some extent unconsciously, their ability to confront their counterparts on the other side when it became clear that the EU negotiators were quite intransigent on the main questions.

The second mistake was to assume that, in the wake of the referendum, the EU would try to facilitate Britain's withdrawal from the union with a minimum of disruption on both sides. But what the

British failed to appreciate was that the EU is viewed, at least by the French and Germans, not as some kind of loose confederation of nation states but as a supra-national body with an almost theological quality. On this view an attempt to leave the union is akin to heresy by the member of a church and deserving of the most severe penalties. It was in this vein that the president of the EU said in February that those in Britain who supported Brexit deserve “a special place in hell”. And the President of the European Commission has described former British prime minister, David Cameron, who called the referendum as “one of the great destroyers of modern times.” In the past when some EU members voted against changes to the union’s constitution, the EU simply ignored the vote and resubmitted the proposal until the electorate gave in and accepted it. Why would it accept the result of the British vote?

The third mistake, closely aligned to the second was to effectively rule out from the start the option of leaving the EU without any kind of deal between the two sides. This took a lot of pressure of the EU negotiators who did not have to face up to the possibility that, if they did not formulate a realistic proposal for the terms of exit, they might face a result that was just as unpredictable for them as it was for Britain.

The fourth mistake was to allow the EU to introduce the false issue of the border between the Irish republic and the British province of Northern Ireland and then insist that there could be no customs posts on the border. Why not has never been explained. Some EU members obviously have borders with countries that are not part of the union and presumably there is not the same free flow of trade and people as exists between EU members. The notion that some kind of border control between the two separate countries that form parts of the Irish landmass would spark some kind of return to terrorist activities in Northern Ireland seems without rational basis. But the EU’s demands on this issue have been used to block any agreement with the British government almost from the start of the negotiations.

This is not, of course, the first time the Irish border has infected British politics and brought it to a standstill. In 1914 the question of whether Northern Ireland should be excluded from legislation proposing Irish home rule had brought the United Kingdom to the brink of civil discord and this prospect was only averted by the outbreak of the Great War in August of that year.

The fifth mistake was to treat the EU negotiators as representative of twenty-seven different countries. There are twenty-seven countries in the union but it is effectively dominated by France and Germany. It might have been more effective to negotiate directly with these two and leave them to explain any settlement to the others. Such a course can hardly have achieved a worst result that has occurred to date.

The truth is that the referendum result flew in the face of enormously powerful groups in Britain and in Europe who were never going to accept it. But their goal of reversing the result has certainly been made more likely by the incompetence with which the British government has conducted the negotiations with the EU.

THE AUSTRALIAN

Wednesday, September 18, 2019

PLENTY OF SPANNERS THROWN INTO THE BREXIT WORKS

Westminster principle extinguished along with the right of the people to choose

The spectacle of Boris Johnson being booed by demonstrators in Luxembourg yesterday is a reminder that the result of the Brexit referendum in 2016 has never been accepted by many forces in the European Union and in Britain itself. And one of those forces is the British parliament which has tried to destroy the government's negotiating position with the European Union by denying the option of a no-deal Brexit while at the same time voting against the government's proposal for a general election that would resolve the impasse between the executive and legislative branches.

Common sense dictates that, if the executive and the parliament cannot agree on a major issue, the parliament has lost confidence in the government and there has to be an election. Just because the opposition groups – Labour, Liberal Democrats and Scottish Nationals – will not formally move a vote of no-confidence can hardly mean that this basic principle of the Westminster political system does not apply.

As for the parliament's demand that a further extension be sought from the EU, if the parliament wants this demand to be met, it has a simple solution. It can agree to an election and, if the opposition forces are successful in that election, they can seek an extension from the EU. The conduct of negotiations with foreign powers has always been one of the functions of the executive government and cannot realistically be taken over by the legislative body.

All this is no doubt a source of great pleasure to the EU bureaucrats in Brussels who have sabotaged the negotiating process from its outset, being determined to secure a reversal of the referendum vote if possible or otherwise to punish Britain for its temerity in trying to leave this supra-national body.

One of the most successful tactics employed by the EU in undermining the Brexit process has been the creation of the false issue of the Irish border. The EU has existing borders with non-members, most obviously Switzerland, and this does not seem to have caused a problem. The idea that some kind of customs formalities on the border between the Irish republic and Northern Ireland would cause a return to civil conflict seems far-fetched. As it happens, the original conflict was instigated by IRA terrorists who do not recognise the existence of Northern Ireland as a separate country. It must be doubted whether questions of customs and excise are of any great concern to them.

Although it is quite right to point to the bloody-mindedness of the EU over the last three years since the referendum in Britain, it must be said that the conduct of the negotiations on the British side has been hopeless. The concept of a no-deal Brexit needed to be introduced at the very start by the British side so that the possible consequences of their intransigence could be brought home to the EU negotiators. One of the reasons why this did not happen was because, until very recently, the British negotiators were largely persons who never wanted Brexit to happen either and thought that the electorate had made a terrible mistake when they voted for it.

This whole exercise has been something of a study in the power and resilience of the public and private institutions outside government but underpinning the modern state. In the face of opposition to Brexit from the political class, the bureaucracy and almost all of the media, the referendum vote has counted for little. These groups have simply refused to accept it and they have no secret of their contempt for the views of the electorate.

One of their tactics has been a series of court cases, the current one being brought to argue that the proroguing of parliament was illegal. Such a claim could never be successful in Australia – and should not be in Britain – because this is an issue over which the courts traditionally have no jurisdiction.

The importance of Brexit is not really about issues like trade and immigration. It is a question of national sovereignty, that is, whether Britain is ultimately to be ruled from Westminster or from Brussels. It may suit the other members of the EU to be provinces of a supra-national body that is largely controlled by France and Germany but that is not the history of Britain and a majority of those who voted at the referendum three years ago seem to have understood that membership of the EU is basically inconsistent with many centuries as an independent nation.

THIS SPORTING LIFE

If ever there was a lost cause, it is reflected in these articles which question the large role of government, especially the federal government, in Australia's major sporting codes. Influenced by significant financial support, the codes have accepted various regulatory regimes, most particularly an intrusive system designed to penalise the use of some – although not all – performance-enhancing substances. I made the argument that this was not a role for governments, given the substantial resources that these bodies have to manage their own affairs but, as already noted, legislation regulating sporting activities continues to increase year by year.

THIS SPORTING LIFE

AUSTRALIAN

Monday, August 3, 2009

NATIONAL COVERAGE WILL OFFER A KICK START

The cost of putting a second AFL club into Sydney will be recouped by TV revenue

The decision by the AFL to establish a second team in Sydney in 2012 has provoked considerable scepticism from many commentators. They have pointed to the relatively flimsy support base of the one existing team – the Swans – and the fact that the code has always struggled to capture the enthusiasm of the Sydney sporting community. But they have largely failed to understand the object of this exercise.

It remains true, that in four of the six States and in the Northern Territory the AFL is the dominant football code by a large margin. And its Queensland experiment with the Brisbane Lions has been quite successful, even though Queensland remains one of the two strongholds of the NRL. In these circumstances New South Wales is crucial to a truly national competition and to the countrywide television grid that produces the AFL's largest source of revenue. It follows that the costs of putting a second team into Sydney – which will be enormous – are likely to be recouped by the sale of television rights, just as the heavy subsidisation of the Swans over many years has achieved the same result.

In any event, Sydney cannot be compared as a sporting market with any of the other capitals. As in so many other respects, it is quite different from the rest of the country. No football code has the support in Sydney that AFL has in most parts of Australia but there are a number of reasons for this.

One point that needs to be made about attendances at sporting events in Sydney is that most of these events are very difficult to attend. The size of the city, combined with its acute traffic problems and lack of a comprehensive system of public transport, means that games at the Sydney Cricket Ground and the Sydney Football Stadium, for example, are simply out of reach for much of the population. The Olympic Stadium at Homebush is more central to the distribution of people in the metropolitan area but even it has seldom had large crowds.

Another factor that is significant in Sydney is its sharper social divisions, particularly reflected in the separate worlds of Rugby Union and Rugby League. Union has its heartland on the lower North Shore and its financial base in the corporate world. Its player and supporter core is the tight-knit world of Sydney's private boys' schools. Its club games draw very small crowds and even the Super 14 fixtures are not shown on free-to-air-television. Only the two or three international games each year are a sell-out and it is something of a mystery where all these additional fans come from. But there is no shortage of money and the players are probably the highest paid of any of the codes, partly, of course, because there are fewer of them at the top level.

League, on the other hand, is now largely a game for television, with relatively small attendances but still a strong tribal loyalty in a number of parts of Sydney. It was originally seen as a working class sport. That concept has little meaning today but there would still not be much cross-over between those regularly attending Union and League fixtures. The NRL has done well in its sale of the television rights to a code that is essentially confined to two States, although coverage is very heavily oriented towards the large Sydney market.

Soccer has lifted its profile considerably in recent years, particularly in Sydney and Melbourne which have very large ethnic communities. These still form the code's regular support base for matches in the A League. As a consequence, there has not been great scope to date for the sale of television rights, although the qualifying games for the World Cup involving the Australian team have been shown and reached a wider audience.

One factor about the Swans' role in Sydney that is seldom mentioned in AFL circles – perhaps not surprisingly – is the team's very unattractive style of play. In contrast to the fast, open and attacking game that some teams have developed, the Swans spend most of their time trying to close the play down. They don't score many goals themselves but try to restrict the other side's opportunities. They have been greatly assisted in this by the size of the SCG which is too short for AFL and leaves little space for open football. It is true that the Swans won the flag in 2005 but they are certainly no fun to watch and they are unlikely to capture the imagination of anyone who is not already a dedicated supporter.

All this suggests that putting a second AFL team into Sydney is going to be very difficult and expensive exercise. But the AFL will be aware that the Sydney market poses particular problems for all its competitors as well. It will also know that, whatever attendances at the actual games may be, the costs can probably be recouped from the sale of the viewing rights to what will be the only football code with a complete national coverage.

THE AUSTRALIAN

Thursday, February 14, 2013

IT MAY NOT BE FAIR PLAY BUT IS IT REALLY ILLEGAL

Why has the federal government got massively involved in drugs in sport?

It would be hard to find more confusing coverage of an issue than that over the last week of drugs in sport. Much of this confusion centres around the term "illegal".

There are, of course, a range of performance-enhancing substances that are banned by the Australian Sports Anti-Doping Authority (ASADA) and the World Anti-Doping Authority (WADA). But that is not a legal regime. It is based on the willingness of the major commercial sporting bodies, particularly the football codes, to voluntarily impose suspensions on competitors who are found, as a result of testing, to have used the banned drugs.

There are, however, ways in which the use of performance-enhancing substances such as peptides, may be contrary to law and so "illegal" – if, for example, it is:

- a prohibited import under the federal Customs Act;
- a legal import but only able to be used under medical prescription which was not provided;
- used under a fraudulent medical prescription.

There is also the category of so-called recreational drugs, such as cannabis and cocaine, whose possession or use is a criminal offence under State law. They are, however, also the subject of testing by ASADA and a positive finding can result in suspension for the player in question.

The most puzzling question in all of this is how performance-enhancing substances came to be an area of massive federal regulation. ASADA is a body established by Commonwealth legislation and funded by taxpayers. The AFL and NRL, like the other major football codes and the governing bodies of tennis and cricket in Australia, are private businesses with substantial revenues, particularly from sponsorship and media rights. They are presumably quite capable of regulating drug use within their sports if they wish to do so. The answer from Canberra would no doubt be that the federal government puts a lot of money into all major sports in Australia, including 300 million dollars towards the team that was sent to the London Olympics last year. It is possible to be a sports fan, however, and still question whether this is a proper use of the limited pool of taxpayer's dollars.

The lengthy investigation by the Australian Crime Commission is another aspect of the role of federal government in this area. If there is significant evidence of match-fixing – itself a criminal offence – or the role of organised crime, the Commission is entitled to be involved. But it is not easy to see what its concern would be with breaches of ASADA's code of conduct. The Commission said in its report that it had "identified significant issues in professional and sub-elite sport in Australia which undermine the principles of fair play". What has fair play got to do with criminal law?

All this raises another important question. In a world where everything done by elite athletes is designed to enhance their performance, why single out a limited range of drugs from all other supplements and techniques? This is an area where the difference between a permitted and non-permitted training supplement – categories devised by ASADA – can be highly marginal.

If there were no such restrictions, presumably there would be a level playing field because everyone would have access to the same regimes. There would, of course, be an issue for individuals, given the fact that the use of some drugs, such as anabolic steroids, can have permanently harmful effects if taken in sufficient quantities. It is also true that these drugs are much more useful in some sports are much more useful in some sports, for example, cycling, than in others, for example, tennis.

On the subject of cycling, it demonstrates the notion of the level playing field. It is not necessary to like Lance Armstrong, who seems to be a particularly unpleasant character, to know that almost all of his major competitors would have been taking the same banned substances as he was. So the net result was that most of the riders in the Tour de France were in the same position and the results probably reflect their relative capacities.

As already noted, professional sportsmen and women are tested not only for banned substances but also for recreational drugs. But why should bodies like ASADA and WADA be concerned with this? If the athlete's performance is affected by the use of, for example, cannabis, this is a problem for the individual or for his or her team mates in group sports. As for the notion of role models, the lives of professional athletes are now so removed from the general community that it is hard to imagine anyone being influenced by their conduct. There might be an argument that some people are influenced by the conduct of movie stars. But they are not tested for drug use or for anything else, being one of the few sectors of society not subject to extensive government regulation.

THE AUSTRALIAN

Friday, August 16, 2013

END THIS BIZARRE DRUGS IN SPORT REGIME

The heavy-handed regulation of the federal government should be dismantled

In late July Jonathan Thurston, probably the single best rugby league player in the country, was awoken at 6am in his Townsville home by a knock on the door. It was a team of officials from the Australian Sports Drug Agency come to do a drug test. What on earth is going on here? Why is a taxpayer-funded federal government agency policing the use of training aids by professional sportsmen and sportswomen?

The issue of drugs in sport became big news in February of this year when two federal ministers and the chief executive of the Australian Crime Commission held a press conference to preside over "the blackest day in the history of Australian sport". No one has ever explained why a national law enforcement body was investigating the use of sports supplements rather than serious criminal activity.

The next step in the saga was the investigation by ASADA of the AFL and the NRL, focused on two clubs – Essendon in the AFL and Cronulla in the NRL. In the course of the NRL investigation – still unfinished – ASADA has already interviewed over 150 persons and examined 55,000 documents. Its report on Essendon is over 400 pages and refers to 13,000 documents. No one has ever explained the establishment and continued existence of a statutory body designed to regulate the affairs of private sporting organisations. Although the federal government has no constitutional power in relation to sport, bodies like the AFL and the NRL have accepted federal funding and signed up to the ASADA regime. But that would not have happened without Canberra's decision to involve government in the world of sport. The AFL and the NRL have huge revenues from the sale of media rights and would be more than capable of regulating the use of performance-enhancing substances by their players with their own resources.

And what were the conclusions of the 400 page report of the Essendon investigation? No players were named as having taken banned substances but failures of administration by various officials were apparently identified – a matter of no obvious concern to ASADA – and are to be the subject of charges by the AFL, which will be fought in the courts by Essendon.

Putting aside the question of the safety of some performance-enhancing drugs – which is a matter for medical advice – there seems to be an arbitrary distinction between those drugs that are on the banned list of the World Anti-Doping Authority, which is the list adopted by ASADA, and those that are not, given that presumably almost everything consumed by a professional athlete is in some way performance-enhancing. This has been illustrated by the dispute over whether AOD-9604 – the drug at the heart of the Essendon investigation – was on the WADA banned list or not. This was a substance designed – unsuccessfully – to treat obesity and then apparently used to promote the repair of cartilage and muscle tissue after injury.

The hysteria that has marked the conduct of the ACC and ASADA in this area was reflected in the ACC proposal that there be a federal criminal offence – punishable by at least three years' imprisonment – for supplying a person with a substance that was on the WADA banned list. As for ASADA, it pushed for – and got – increased powers in the last days of the federal parliamentary sitting before its finishing prior to the election. These legislative changes allow ASADA to require a person to provide documents or face a fine of $5,100, potentially for every day the documents are not produced. A document must be produced even if its contents would tend to incriminate the person producing it and it can also be used in any proceedings before a sports tribunal. ASADA can also require a person to attend an interview to answer questions, unless the answers may be incriminating, with the same penalty for a refusal to answer. It would not, of course, be possible to apply this kind of regime to a person charged with a serious criminal offence. Yet it has been imposed by this legislation on persons whose conduct may not be illegal in any respect.

Why regulation of drugs in sport became such a big industry in Australia and was taken over by the federal government is something of a puzzle, although, as in so many other areas, the proper role of government in this country is never discussed. In the US the recent investigation that ended with suspensions being handed down to some of baseball's most famous players was conducted entirely by Major League Baseball. Admittedly, Congress held hearings on the state of America's "national pastime" in the 2000s, but no legislation was passed, and many people questioned whether Congress should hold such hearings, or even had the legal power to do so. It is the lack of questioning in the Australian context that is remarkable.

It would be attractive to think that whoever takes office in Canberra after 7 September would dismantle this bizarre regime but recent history tells us that the scope of government regulation is never scaled back but only increased.

THE AUSTRALIAN

Monday, June 23, 2014

ABOLISH ASADA AND GET CANBERRA OUT OF SPORT

The anti-doping authority's coercive powers exceed anything available to the police

The so-called "blackest day in Australian sport" occurred on 7 February 2013 in the form of a press conference by two federal ministers and the chief executive of the Australian Crime Commission, flanked by the heads of Australia's major sporting bodies who had been summoned to attend. "We will catch you", said Sports Minister, Kate Lundy, "Come forward before you get a knock at the door", said Home Affairs Minister, Jason Clare.

Almost a year and a half later the Australian Sports Anti-Doping Agency has issued notices to 34 present and former players at AFL Club Essendon alleging the use of a peptide know as Thymosin Beta 4. The report of ASADA's investigation of Essendon was more than 400 pages and based on 8,500 transcript pages of interviews. According to ASADA, its investigations into Essendon and NRL Club Cronulla involved 280 interviews and the consideration of 120,000 documents. All this material was then in turn reviewed early in 2014 by retired Federal Court Judge Garry Downes to consider what action should be taken as a result.

It is now almost forgotten that the Crime Commission report released at the February 2013 press conference was entitled "Organised Crime and Drugs in Sport". Despite this sensationalist title, it contained only the vaguest references to the role of criminal groups in supplying performance enhancing drugs to sports competitors and no more has ever been heard on this subject from the Crime Commission.

ASADA's inquiries, conducted at public expense by a federal statutory body, are not concerned with drugs that are illegal under the criminal law but with substances that ASADA and its international counterpart, the World Anti-Doping Authority, consider should not be used by sporting participants. In the absence of any issues about the safe use of the substances, this is an arbitrary classification scheme. There are, of course, a wide range of performance-enhancing dietary materials and training regimes that are not on the banned list of ASADA or WADA. It might be assumed that almost everything that a professional athlete does is designed to improve his or her performance so it is hard to see why some of these procedures are considered unfair but others not.

Under the legislation establishing ASADA it has coercive powers to summon and interrogate sports men and women with a fine of $5,100 a day for failure to attend and for a refusal to answer questions, unless the answer may be incriminating. These powers far exceed those available to the police in relation to persons charged with serious criminal offences.

No one has ever explained how the federal government came to have this role in the world of sport. It certainly has no constitutional power in this area and it is hard to see what these activities have to do with the traditional functions of government. It is true that the major sporting codes, including the AFL and the NRL, have voluntarily signed up to the ASADA regime but this was essentially the result of pressure from Canberra. There is no shortage of funds in these bodies, chiefly from the sale of media rights, that would enable them to establish their own systems of drug regulations if they wanted to do so.

The abolition of ASADA would, of course, be a cost-saving measure for the federal government and that might be considered a good thing in the current state of the budget. But the real reason why ASADA should be abolished is that it is a classic example of government regulation of an activity that has never had and still has no connection with the role of government. If the various sporting codes choose to regulate the use of performance-enhancing substances in their own field, that is a matter for them. But then it would not be a matter for public servants and the taxpayers who support them.

It is likely, however, that the costs of ASADA's investigations into Essendon and Cronulla have only just started. The notices served on the Essendon players will almost certainly trigger a lengthy legal process in tribunals and courts and the same will be true in the case of Cronulla players if, as expected, notices are served on some of them. One inevitable consequence of government regulation in any area is that it provides a new field of work for lawyers. In the case of ASADA, it has proved already to be a bonanza for the legal profession.

THE AUSTRALIAN

Thursday, January 14, 2016

PUZZLING QUESTION FOR SPORT

The AFL has paid a very heavy price in signing up to the WADA rules

As a lifelong Geelong supporter, I never thought I would say a good word about the Essendon Football Club. But the judgment of the court of arbitration in sport raises the question of how two international bodies have been able to destroy for the immediate future one of the oldest clubs in the AFL.

The CAS was established in 1984 and was the brainchild of then Olympic president, Juan Antonio Samaranch. The case against the Essendon players was conducted by the World Anti-Doping Authority. It might be noted that the CAS verdict decided an appeal from an AFL tribunal, presided over by a retired Victorian judge, which found that there was insufficient evidence to establish that the Essendon players had been injected with a banned substance.

The point should be made, however, that the substance in question – a peptide apparently used to promote the repair of muscle tissue after injury – is not an illegal drug. It is simply on a list that WADA considers should not be used. The list is quite arbitrary because there are a whole range of performance-enhancing substances and training regimes that are not banned. It might be assumed that every aspect of the life of an elite sportsman or sportswoman is designed to enhance their performance.

This is not to say that some drugs may not raise a medical issue. Anabolic steroids, for example, can be damaging if taken in large quantities over a lengthy period of time. But this is not the basis for

WADA's list of banned substances.

It is not even necessary that the drugs for which athletes are now tested have any connection with sporting performance. The Australian Sports Anti-Doping Authority tests for the presence of drugs such as cannabis and cocaine, although their use or possession is a criminal offence and so can be dealt with by this area of the law.

What has happened over the last two decades is that the supervision of drugs in sport has become a huge world-wide industry, supporting an army of zealous bureaucrats and sporting officials. This is reflected in Australia by the existence of a federal statutory body in the form of ASADA that is funded by taxpayers to engage in these activities. Under its legislation ASADA can require persons to attend for interviews and produce documents or face a fine of $5,100 for every day the documents are not produced. Someone charged with a serious criminal offence could not be subjected to this kind of regime.

If this involvement by governments in private sector sporting competitions is curious, how much more puzzling is the fact that the bodies administering these competitions have signed up to the WADA system and placed the fate of their players – and to some extent themselves – in the hands of international organisations over which they have no control?

There is no doubt that the AFL and other major sporting bodies were subjected to considerable pressure by federal governments to subscribe to the WADA code. But the question is why did they agree? It is true that many of these sporting bodies receive some funding from the federal government but the recent sale of television rights by the AFL suggests that it could survive very well without government grants. The real reason seems to be that the major sporting bodies see themselves very much as part of the Australian establishment and proper partners for governments in a number of policy areas. If so, the AFL has paid a very heavy price for this view of its public role.

One of its teams has been effectively wiped out for the competition for 2016 with the result that one game in every round is likely to be a dead rubber with dismal consequences for match attendances and television ratings.

The WADA regime is naturally a great boon for lawyers and has sparked a vast amount of litigation in numerous countries over the years. Essendon is reported to have spent $7 million on its defence case. ASADA's report on Essendon ran to more than 400 pages and referred to 13,000 documents. It is now possible that all the suspended players may sue Essendon in civil proceedings because they will lose a year in what is by definition a relatively short playing career.

All this suggests that government and sport is a bad mix but, as in so many areas in Australia, the lines between the public and private sectors have become increasingly difficult to draw.

www.ingramcontent.com/pod-product-compliance
Lightning Source LLC
Chambersburg PA
CBHW060237100726
47907CB00003B/677

* 9 7 8 1 9 2 2 4 4 9 0 0 9 *